The Fury

Also by JoAnn Fastoff

Fiction
Howard Watson Intrigue Series
>*The Avaricious*
>*The Scheduler*
>*The Standing People*
>*The Smoke Ring*
>*The Lie*
>*The Pact*
>*The Gordian Knot*

Non-Fiction
You Play Like A Girl
(History of the first Women in Sports)
White Sox
(and other baseball worth mentioning) *for Women*
Two Years of Heaven
(Stories of re-kindled Happiness)

As a university criminal justice professor (including teaching courses on espionage and terrorism), and a former FBI Special Agent, I am a stickler for accurate details. Absent them I lose interest quickly as it indicates a lack of sufficient research. In *The Fury, A Howard Watson Intrigue*, JoAnn Fastoff's accurate descriptions and details throughout heightened my enjoyment of the book. I loved this book and am confident future readers will as well....especially those who value attention to detail and a fast, flowing, and exciting story they can immerse themselves in.

Dr. Walter N. Clements, PhD, CPP
The Clements Group LLC
Former FBI Special Agent

In JoAnn Fastoff's book, *The Fury, A Howard Watson Intrigue*, past perceived transgressions rears its ugly head. Howard Watson is back on duty and this time it's personal. Very personal! In this thrilling read, rogue FBI Agents and CIA intelligence officers set off a chain reaction 14 years prior leading up to today. You won't want to miss out on what happens. Highly recommended.

R. Lee Walters
Former FBI Special Agent (1989-2012)

JoAnn Fastoff continues her fast-paced, FBI-based series in fine form. In *The Fury, A Howard Watson Intrigue*, the action is non-stop, but Fastoff blends in a very human element that adds to the enjoyment of her latest work. I truly enjoyed reading this.

James Treacy
Retired FBI Special Agent/SSA

The Fury is a must-read for all fans of thriller/crime fiction. JoAnn Fastoff's ability to combine personal drama along with societal issues makes for a compelling read. Her fans will appreciate being able to continue with the *Howard Watson Intrigue* series. Other readers will be excited to discover a new favorite author.

Paige Lovitt
for Reader Views

The Fury
(A Howard Watson Intrigue)

JoAnn Fastoff

To you, who have always believed in me.

Philadelphia, PA

Spring Garden, a neighborhood consisting of both residences and cultural attractions, includes historic Museum Row and upper-class Boathouse Row. The residential areas are composed mostly of three-story brownstones built during the late 19th century.

Although it was pouring rain Shari Stover could still make out the east bank of the Schuylkill River from her third-floor bedroom window. However, the usually beautiful view took a backseat to the phone call that announced her former husband had died in prison. She should have been happy with this news, but the rage she had been feeling for fourteen years finally boiled over.

When her husband went to prison, he left her financially bankrupt due to all the lawyer fees. Besides her full-time supervisory nursing job, Shari had to work a side hustle to pay for therapy for their two children, Joel and Gina, which still didn't help *her.* Thank God she had saved *some* money, but it wasn't enough.

She was humiliated. She was disgraced. She was ostracized. So much so that she went back to her maiden name and, in the process, changed her children's last names too. They moved as far away from Washington, DC as her wallet would permit. She hated the FBI for allowing her husband to stray. She especially hated FBI Special Agent Howard Watson.

***

Seven miles north of her mother's house and attending Temple University, Gina Stover, now a college junior, reflected on the news that her father was dead. For fourteen years, she only knew him as the greedy, lying snake that made her family's life miserable for years. Perhaps now her mom could exhale.

***

Across the Schuylkill River, the two-story glass and aluminum building hosting the name *Carlton & Associates Accounting* wrapped around a square block. The third largest accounting firm in Philadelphia took great pleasure in hiring what they believed to be the most innovative accounting majors from the best schools in the country.

Joel Stover stepped away from his office window on the second floor. He mulled over the fact that his father had died. He was finally dead and, therefore, could no longer bring misery to his mother's life. Now that he was grown and moved away, Joel felt it was time to settle a debt with Howard Watson. He would start with Watson's wife.

"In getting even, what price is paid?"

PART ONE

FBI Washington Field Office, Washington, DC

Assistant Director-in-Charge (ADIC) was the lettering on Alberto Marino's door. He was staring at the lifeless looking flags trying desperately to wave on the poles outside his third-floor big picture window. He sighed. Not because the rain outside was coming down in buckets but because he was expecting freshly-minted Special Agents to absorb completely in one hour what his division was responsible for and what it had accomplished, especially under his fifteen-year reign. Marino suddenly felt old as the three newly graduated agents were ushered into his conference room. He was only fifty-five, but the fresh and eager faces staring at him for tons of advice made him feel even older. *Where is Howard, Frank, and Archie when I need them?*

Fortunately, the questions were never challenging. The rookies always had the same questions and were given the same answers. Although Marino and the other Assistant Directors enjoyed these intermittent exercises, mainly devised to keep them on their toes, they always seemed to come at the most inconvenient time…which to Marino was pretty much all the time. It was reassuring to Marino to see a person of color in the group, although the agency was still lagging in hiring female agents.

He would later call his three Supervisory Special Agents and drill them relentlessly as to where they were when he was conducting this kindergarten class on how to stay alive. At his level, this was really an exercise for his supervisors. However, if the FBI taught him anything, it was "Morale and leadership matter. Employees with a shortage of the former will work less hard and collaborate less effectively." He was ready for these young snots.

The first question out of the box from the rookie from Kentucky had to do with Marino's first day on the job. Marino thought about it for a moment because he couldn't recall being asked this question in the past ten years.

"On my first day in the Atlanta Field Office," he began, "my supervisor handed me his car keys and told me to figure out where the U.S. Attorney's Office was as well as the rest of the city of Atlanta because he didn't want to see me in the office any more than necessary."

The agents laughed. Then the regular barrage of questions came on like a snowball down a hill. Thirty minutes later the agents went back to their respective field divisions. Marino took a cigar from his desk drawer and ran it slowly across his upper lip. He then put it back in its humidor and summoned his three supervisory agents.

Philadelphia, PA

Although it was raining heavily, Janet Forrestal could not feel happier. She was exuberant about her baby boy, due in three weeks, and her baby shower in three days. She was extremely pleased that the FBI had finally emerged into the twenty-first century and granted her *paid* parental leave when she was ready to spit out the kid. She thought life was *too* perfect. Her husband Allen told her, "Stop thinking like that; the worse is over. I've recovered from my injuries; the baby seems to be healthy, all his fingers and toes are attached where they're supposed to be, and we are doing fine. Leave it alone!"

But, of course, as a first-time mother-to-be, she was being overly cautious. Thank God she had her mom and her friend Carol Watson, who would both steer her clear of crushing thoughts. Carol was her hero—someone married to another Leo (law enforcement officer) *and* a mother who knew life from many angles.

FBI Washington Field Office

It was noon, and Howard Watson, FBI Supervisory Special Agent (SSA), was really hungry. He had met earlier with a private law enforcement group to discuss various safety mechanisms to ensure they were legal. Howard thought the group would have more than just coffee—he was wrong—so now he was really hungry. He glanced at the rain beating on his window, thinking it would stop if he kept looking at it, but no such luck. He didn't want to eat in the employee cafeteria because it was spring in DC, which meant flowers were blooming and trees were turning bright pink and white, and, "get real, Watson, outside cafes will be back after this miserable winter."

Again, no such luck with the rain.

His second-floor window faced the inner courtyard of the building. The employees seated outside dashed to get back inside the building from the unannounced rain. Howard chuckled, as he always enjoyed watching staff dart like mice whenever there was a sudden downpour.

The rain beating on his window had almost placed Howard in a trance. He was brought back to the world several moments later when his Assistant Program Analyst walked into his office to inform him that a former Special Agent, Eric Glenn, had died in federal prison. "Damn!" was all Howard could say. After serving a fourteen-year sentence, Glenn had only a week left behind bars.

Glenn's prostate cancer, Howard learned, could have been prevented from spreading, but Glenn refused any treatment.

Howard now turned his attention to the thought of his wife Carol who had survived Glenn's gunshot wound those fourteen years ago. Should he call her and tell her of this latest unfolding or wait until after she returned from the baby shower next weekend in Philly? He decided he would wait. Right now, he was on his way to a meeting in Marino's office to welcome a female to his team—Sandra Callahan.

***

When Howard arrived, his unit—Tim Yamamoto, Ahmad Waverly, Brett Hamilton, and Kevin Lee—were already seated. Callahan was slightly late but strolled through the doors as if she belonged inside. Today she did. She was now part of Howard Watson's team. Howard knew Marino did not want a female under his thumb. Hell, it was hard enough with the various men assembled. And, she was feisty. He hated that in a woman. But Marino couldn't ignore Callahan's determination, perseverance, and the fact that she dogged Howard for the past year to join his team. Marino brought the assemblage to order.

"Men…sorry…agents, today we welcome someone who has proven herself in many ways that she belongs with our unit. I hope you all feel the same about her qualifications and our reasons for allowing her to join us. Welcome, SSA Sandra Callahan."

The applause was not only thunderous, it was legitimate. Callahan rose to thank everyone in the room. As she was about to speak, John Fleischman, Deputy Director, walked into the room. Callahan immediately sat down.

"Agents, sorry, I'm tardy," he said almost sincerely. "Al, if you don't mind my saying a few words?"

Marino nodded for him to take his usual stage.

"The FBI has long held that women couldn't handle the physical rigors of the special agent position, which includes making arrests, taking part in raids, and engaging in self-defense. Those days, I am proud to say, are in the past. Times are changing, and I'm happy to announce that females are taking on more demanding positions, physically and otherwise."

Howard glanced over at Marino with a look of *where is he going with this?*

Fleischman continued to spew history, especially the history Marino sent him the previous evening. "Today, we have 2,675 women Special Agents, serving on and leading counterterrorism squads, cyber squads, counterintelligence squads, covert operations teams, and criminal squads. They head field offices, including the largest in the Bureau—New York. They work as firearm instructors and in all other specialty fields both domestically and international. They are superb agents who happen to be women."

Marino was quite pleased that Fleischman had memorized his notes.

"So I, along with Al, Howard, and the rest of Howard's unit," he continued, "want to welcome you, SSA Sandra Callahan, because you have certainly proven your worth to us and all the FBI."

Again the applause was thunderous. Fleischman then shook Callahan's hand, nodded to the just arrived photographer, posed for the requisite picture with Marino, Howard, and Callahan and departed. Shortly after that, Wendy, Marino's EA, wheeled in the cake, coffee, and cards. The four secretaries also joined in the celebration.

"Callahan," Marino said to her matter-of-factly, "now you're just one of the guys, got it?"

"Got it, Director," she answered.

"Oh God," Marino bellowed, "you can call me Al." Laughter filled the room.

Dulles Airport, Washington, DC

Carol Watson felt honored to fly to Philadelphia to host Janet's baby shower. She easily saw Janet as the little sister she always wanted, adding to the two brothers her parents bestowed upon her without her consent. Seated next to her on the plane was their good friend Kelly Yamamoto, who was being reminded on this girl's trip that she was leaving her two-year-old son with his father. Kelly told Carol that her husband "would have to sink or swim." The laughter lasted probably longer than it should have, but both women knew it wasn't long enough. Across the aisle was Liling Xu, a colleague of Janet's husband and a trusted friend to them all.

This baby shower Carol thought was going to be the ultimate adventure. As she looked back on her life, she remembered another time on an airplane–

14 years ago –

Carol and her then ten-year-old son Mark were about to board a plane from Chicago to DC, and Mark had freaked out because he had left his late grandfather's baseball glove in the airport restaurant where they were eating. Once on the plane, Mark was inconsolable, so much so that he ran off the plane, and Carol had to chase him through the airport, where he found the glove in the chair where he had left it. She would have scolded him, except that he broke down and cried because that was the only thing he had left of his grandfather, and he didn't want to lose it…she remembered holding him close. Carol also remembered the plane they missed…exploded after takeoff.

***

Carol shuddered at the memory because she couldn't believe it was fourteen years ago. *Almost a lifetime, but sometimes feels like yesterday.* The chatter of her friends brought her back to the present.

14 years ago–

Eric Glenn liked the idea of being an FBI Agent. He

wanted all the perks: an agency-issued car, a decent salary and a good benefits package, and travel opportunities. He also liked that agents were paid much more than local law enforcement, mostly because education requirements were higher in the FBI. He could draw on resources that were orders of magnitude greater than any local law enforcement department. And in the areas of search and seizure, use of informants, wiretapping, second-party recording, etc., federal law and regulations were less restrictive as an FBI Agent.

Yes, Eric Glenn liked his job. Of course, his wife and children detested the long hours, having only some weekends and holidays off, and always, always being available 24/7. Glenn was always ready. So when approached by two CIA officers to retrieve a microchip from a special agent in Chicago, Glenn only asked how much? With the figure offered, it became easy to talk his partner, David Snell, into the scheme.

Glenn never figured anyone would get killed, but someone did kill the Chicago Special Agent and someone did kill the agent's colleague, a decorated retired Army veteran. Nowhere in the plan did he ever believe he would be personally responsible for injuring the Chicago agent's wife!

In exchange for a lighter sentence, Glenn and his partner David Snell had informed the US Attorney's office of the two CIA officers who had hired them. Glenn then pleaded guilty to two counts of criminal attempt to commit a felony (kidnapping through false pretenses) and assault with a deadly weapon. He received a fourteen-year sentence in federal prison.

***

Sandra Callahan was thrilled to be working in the Washington Field Office, especially on Howard Watson's team. Although her time at the FBI Academy at Quantico, Virginia, was undeniably rewarding, she worked mainly as a weapons and explosives instructor. However, on the flip side, she still learned Bureau operations, forensics, cybercrime, firearms, and law. Quantico constantly updated her on the latest developments in intelligence and she believed these strengths got her through the interview with Alberto Marino.

Callahan was the middle child of two brothers. They were all two years apart, so they were not quite the "Irish triplets." She attended Catholic grammar school and Catholic high school and graduated from the University of Notre Dame, like her father and older brother. She decided to follow a different route for grad school, though, and, to her father's chagrin, chose the University of Chicago. According to her father, U of C was loaded with Jews and WASPs. Sandra didn't care because it was a terrific school and far away from the Callahan family population that seemed to more than double in the Baltimore-DC area.

Sandra thought her father, Daniel, eventually approved of the U of C choice, but as she got closer to moving to Chicago, her mother let her in on a little secret—he wasn't. Although both brothers received pats on their backs when they completed college, she did not. Her father constantly asked her what a woman with degrees in Engineering and French would do with them once she was married?

Daniel Callahan was a hard-headed, well-to-do Irishman who never let Sandra nor her brothers forget where he came from—nothing. However, Sandra readily noticed the difference between her grandfather, Flynn, and his son, Daniel. Flynn pounded the idea of becoming your best by reading and studying. It didn't matter to him if you were a grandson or granddaughter—be the best and be kind. Daniel adhered to this thinking only regarding his sons—not his daughter.

Sandra enjoyed Chicago, especially the Hyde Park area, home to the University of Chicago and the Museum of Science & Industry, with the oldness of the architecture of some of the homes dating back to the Chicago Fire in 1871. The mansions were magnificent, and the new mansions were incredibly modern but needed a personality found only in the older ones. She wasn't crazy about the Chicago winters, but Sandra extended her stay each June to partake in most of Chicago's numerous summer events before heading back to Baltimore.

After grad school, Sandra sought employment in the Baltimore-DC area. Infrastructure Development Engineering hired her a few weeks after graduating to help design and maintain critical infrastructure, specifically bridges and underpasses. After eight months, the company transferred her overseas to their French affiliate, where she could wallow in the French culture all she wanted.

Although she loved the French people and the countryside, the job became boring and too routine, so much so that after two years she transferred back to the States. The love affair lasted only a couple of more months because a disgruntled ex-employee planted a series of bombs throughout the lobby entrance of the company, and no one could enter or leave without the bombs sensing movement and then exploding.

When the FBI bomb squad arrived and finally diffused

the one real bomb, Callahan recognized that only a handful of the two hundred and twenty employees had remained calm. She was one of them. She found the FBI Agents so seemingly in control and so professional in their demeanor that she decided to apply to the Agency. *I need some excitement in my life. This just might be it.*

To say that Daniel Callahan was angry with the news of his only daughter heading to the FBI would be putting it mildly. To say Callahan was furious was closer to the truth. He was so livid that he refused to speak to his daughter for over a week. The "period of ignore" would have lasted longer, except his father Flynn and his wife Bridget refused to speak to him until he apologized to Sandra. Bridget had also showed Daniel the guest bedroom where he would be sleeping.

FBI Philadelphia Field Office, PA

After serving three years in Afghanistan, providing intelligence for the Marines, and being a part of the destruction of al Qaeda and Taliban militant training camps, including the fall of the Taliban government, Katherine "Kat" Perry was ready for domestic law enforcement. When she joined the FBI, she was two classes behind Janet Forrestal's class at Quantico. She had heard about Forrestal's accomplishments from the two female trainees in her class and decided she wanted to be like Janet.

At graduation, no one could be more pleased than Perry after being informed that she would join the Philadelphia Bureau. *In the same division as Janet Forrestal! OMG!* She was pumped and swore to her family that she would not disappoint Janet. Her family members only smiled and shook their heads because Kat never got openly excited about anything, *and* she didn't even know Janet Forrestal!

***

Perry was delighted about attending Janet Forrestal's upcoming baby shower. She and Janet became friendly because they were the only female Intelligence Analysts in the Philly Office and were similar in age. It didn't take long to become friends. Uncomfortable as it was, though, Forrestal had to tell Perry to refrain from trying so hard. "You're worthy," she whispered loudly, "and Philly knows it."

Unfortunately, during Forrestal's leave of absence, Perry would have to share assignments with Gil Holloway, Forrestal's partner. Holloway told her more than once that she "was no Forrestal." She knew this, but did he have to say it more than once? Forrestal mentioned to her before leaving on maternity leave that she and Holloway didn't get along for the first year of their partnership, "so don't expect any miracles and just let the water run down your back."

Perry then asked her superior, Stanton Abrams, if he could pair her with anyone else? He only chuckled and told her there was no one else. "Lump it or leave it."

***

Alberto Marino called his "three-wise-men" supervisory agents into his office: Howard Watson, Frank Leslie, and Archie Jennings.

All three trudged through Marino's oak doors. They knew he would grill them on their sudden disappearance regarding the New Agent Orientation. Howard sat on Marino's chocolate leather sofa while Archie plopped down on one of the empty chairs facing Marino's desk. Frank took a seat at Marino's small conference table.

Marino eyed all three men with a look only a father could give when his sons were about to say, "I didn't do it." But he surprised all three.

"Later this afternoon," he began, "some North America Labor Administration members, or NALA, as they like to be called, will join us in John's office. The issue will be child labor, especially indigenous child labor trafficking in the United States. HQ sent this case to us."

All three men looked surprised.

"Before you question my direction," Marino continued, "I want you to read this document I received this morning. It's called an Issue Paper on child labor." He then handed Archie several documents, who then passed one set to Frank and the other to Howard.

Marino continued. "Seems we are dealing with a company here on the Coast that is allegedly exploiting indigenous children, most of them in manufacturing and agriculture, and this organization, NALA, would like the FBI to take the lead on this case matter to combat the problem."

All three men raised their hands. Marino ignored them.

"I recognize the FBI is not America's police," he said matter-of-factly, "but the American public expects for us to produce results, not excuses. Digest the document, and then you can direct all your questions to NALA at the four p.m. meeting today in John's conference room. That's all."

With Marino's last sentence, all three agents knew Al wasn't going to budge on giving answers. Howard believed he didn't have any.

Deputy Director John Fleischman's conference room

It was still raining when Howard, Frank, and Archie walked into the director's conference room fifteen minutes early. Their moods seemed to match the gloomy weather. Six people were already seated, including Alberto Marino, so the gathering almost made the agents feel like they were late.

"Good. You're all here," Fleischman announced. After introducing Marino's team, he introduced the two men and a woman, representatives from NALA, and a very dark-skinned young man who looked in his early twenties wearing a white shirt that featured the logo of *Baltimore Carrier Bus Lines*. Fleischman gave the NALA woman representative the nod to proceed.

The woman, beautiful by all standards, stood as she greeted those assembled. "Again, I am Georgia Kincaid, and for the past five years I have served as the Executive Director of Operations, responsible for toppling and the ruination of any company in the US that has been charged with the exploitation of children in hazardous occupations."

She paused to put on her eyeglasses and became surprisingly more beautiful.

"Child labor is not an easy topic to talk about. Imagine how it feels when you have facts. A large part of what we do for NALA is to constantly raise awareness about child labor and tell communities, especially underrepresented communities, that children should not work and that they should not do anything other than be allowed to develop as children."

She glanced in the direction of a pitcher of water on the table. Howard recognized he was the closest to the pitcher of water and glasses, so he poured her a drink. All of the men in the room watched her as she sipped from her glass. Kincaid nodded to Howard in an appreciative manner, took several more sips and continued.

"The Issue Paper you received and hopefully read…" She looked around the room. "Shows that child labor and education exclusion among indigenous children form a disproportionately large percentage of hazardous jobs. Most of these jobs are in agriculture but also in construction, manufacturing, and domestic work. Some of you might think this is another form of human trafficking…well, you would be right. Every country is affected. Forced labor in the US generates 150 billion dollars in illicit profits. Consequently American industries and businesses face unfair competition with these under the radar employees, and states lose billions in tax income *and* social security contributions."

She took a deep breath.

Marino stepped to the plate. "Ms. Kincaid, we can see that you are passionate about this subject, and we recognize this is a despicable industry, but how is the FBI in any way able to assist your organization?"

Kincaid introduced the slim, handsome man in the white shirt, who rose slowly from his seat as he adjusted his eyeglasses.

"Good day, I am Amadi Osman. My accent was born in

Sudan, but I have lived in Baltimore for more than seventeen years. My parents brought my sister, brother, and me to the United States when we were young. My father was a tobacco worker in Africa, but his earnings weren't enough to cover the costs of our school supplies and clothes. We came to the US to escape poverty and the tyrannical arm of Sudan's Muslim Brotherhood. I started working during the tobacco harvests in Maryland when I was seven, my brother was eight, and my sister was ten. There didn't seem to be an alternative to our working. My father's employers here in the US told my parents that me and my siblings working in the fields was the only way to make ends meet, which meant our rent, food, water, and clothing. My parents believed in the employers. We realized too late that we traded in one satan in Sudan for another in the US."

He paused. "We would go to school in the winter and work during the summer months of May through August. We would see other children playing while we had to carry on with our work. We worked in the fields, loading and unloading equipment and helping wherever needed. My siblings and I did not get paid. Our parents "traded" our salary for rent. I believe this way the company could say that we didn't work for them and that we were not getting paid."

He adjusted his eyeglasses again.

"I am a driver for the Baltimore Carrier Bus Lines. I drive fifty children to school each day. In the afternoon, I take six of them to an afterschool program near the school, and others pick them up. I believe the building housing the afterschool program is a facade set up by a Foundation called Kelsy-Wahauser, located in the Yorkshire Building. The children going to this afterschool program are Indian, Black, and Mexican. My history has permitted me to see children working hard in construction, in the tobacco fields, as janitors, kitchen helpers, and laundry workers. They might only be eight years old. It reminded me that I know what exploitation looks and feels like. So I went to the Baltimore police, who said they checked the whereabouts of the children and the foundation itself. They, the police, said they went several times to the Yorkshire Building housing the program but found all children either doing afterschool work or on the adjacent playground.

"I now know my naiveté sounded a trumpet. But several times, I noticed these six children the following Mondays, and especially the two girls' hands would have blisters on their palms. I asked where they received the blisters on their hands, and they said, 'Working.' I asked, working on what? They would look down on the ground, not answering, and shake their heads. However, I repeat, I know what exploitation looks like, and these children are in trouble."

He then sat down.

Howard and the rest of the team were speechless. After clearing his throat, John Fleischman brought everyone out of their semi-fog. He managed with a somewhat level of sincerity to inform NALA that one of his fine units would look into this alleged shameful business practice.

Marino held his breath and his tongue.

"Ms. Kincaid," Fleischman asked, "do you have any other witnesses you might want to present to the group that would show or prove beyond a reasonable doubt Mr. Osman's allegations?"

She held in her fury and answered in a hushed tone. "The challenge we face is that in society in general, people think it is normal and right for children to work. We believe this afterschool program in a way we cannot confirm at this time is abusing young children eight to twelve years old by working them secretly behind law enforcement's back. These children are Hispanic and Latino, probably living here under the radar, and Native American and Black children from a so-called orphanage. Mr. Osman was told by some men he had never seen before, that 'they' were watching him and advised him to keep his mouth shut or be ready to be deported. Mr. Osman and his siblings are naturalized citizens. We take—"

"I certainly understand your and Mr. Osman's fear regarding underage children doing laborious work," John Fleischman cut in. "However, if we tell the farmers in this country that their children cannot work with them, most farmers probably would become bankrupt within two years. They believe their children are responsible for keeping the family business, in this case, the family farm afloat."

Howard glanced over at Marino with a look of disgust. Marino shot back *keep calm.*

"Director," Kincaid continued, still without standing but directly looking at him, "farmers make sure their children never work under hazardous conditions because these are children *they* brought into the world. Also, farmers' children work with them, not for them—a completely different scenario."

Fleischman didn't like her tone. However, he straightened his spine not to offer a rebuttal so that she and her party could quickly exit, and he could get back to whatever he was interrupted doing with what he deemed a less-than-factual complaint.

"If I may continue," Kincaid said with no hint of backing down, "three main International Conventions guide the issue of child labor, but in the US, we defer to the United

Nations Convention on the Rights of the Child. These conventions frame the concept of child labor and form the basis for child labor legislation enacted by countries that are signatories. We need the FBI's help to flush out Foundations like Kelsy-Wahauser, and their partners."

The agents were impressed with her grit. Fleischman looked over at Marino, who got the hint.

"Ms. Kincaid," Marino said in an assuring manor, "we will look into these allegations and see where our assistance is needed…if needed."

The four visitors stood up from their chairs, bobbed their heads quickly toward the agents, and were escorted out of the room by Fleischman's EA.

***

The secretary caught Joel Stover as he was leaving his office.

"That package you were looking for, Joel, has arrived."

"Thanks, Gloria," Stover said with no trace of excitement in his voice. "I'm on my way to a meeting, so if you could place it on my desk, I'd appreciate it."

The secretary smiled and walked away.

***14 years ago* –**

Joel Stover was ten when his father, Eric Glenn, was hauled to federal prison. His young mind could not grasp the depth of charges flung at his father. His mom only repeatedly acknowledged they would not see their father for a lengthy time.

It wasn't as if he had enjoyed a warm and nurturing relationship with his father; no, his mother and grandparents made up for that kind of love. Since his father was hardly around, it became more evident to Joel, even at ten, that the most his father could supply in terms of love was his salary and its family benefits. That would suffice and take the place of anything pertaining to love. But when his father went to prison Joel soon realized he and his family became victims of loud whispers behind their backs, looks of disdain, finger-pointing, and smirks so wide it was impossible not to believe they were meant for his family.

He remembered that his mother Shari was distraught for months and that he and his little sister, who was only six at the time, were uprooted from Washington, DC to Philadelphia almost overnight. Looking back, he realized they were poorly treated—from his father's family, his mom's so-called friends, and eventually from his and Gina's friends. Why, he couldn't understand.

He also couldn't understand why his last name was changed from Glenn to Stover. He couldn't understand why his grandparents—his father's parents—constantly reprimanded his mother, telling her it was her fault their son was in trouble, and that if she had been a better wife, he wouldn't have turned to the dark side. These admonishments deflated his mother's morale, which was hard for Joel to bear.

Interestingly, Joel Stover, even with his glasses on, did not see the picture clearly—he was not blaming his father for all the disorder in his life—he was blaming Howard Watson and the FBI who created his father.

***

The package sat on Joel's desk all morning. He stared at it several times before opening it to reveal a pair of gray khaki pants and a matching long-sleeved gray shirt with the logo of Keller's Forest Flowers stitched on the shirt pocket.

He had stared out of his office window for such a lengthy time that his secretary had to cough to let him know she had knocked before she entered his office. In a quiet manner he covered up the uniform and put it in one of the drawers of his desk.

"Joel, sorry to interrupt your train of thought," she exclaimed, "but your meeting with the seniors starts in ten minutes. I brought your figures and documents."

She handed him several papers.

"Thanks, Gloria, you are a lifesaver. Have a good weekend."

He then opened his door to allow her to leave, and he walked down the long hallway to the meeting.

PART TWO

Alberto Marino's office

"Well, what do you think?" Marino asked his supervisors as he lifted out a Coke from his mini refrigerator. He gestured to the three men but each refrained from his offer.

Frank Leslie went first.

"Based on Ms. Kincaid's and Mr. Osman's testimonies, we're more than likely looking at labor trafficking. After checking, we *do* have an international unit called Innocent Images and Crimes Against Children, which, if I'm not mistaken, also jointly works human trafficking."

"I agree with Frank," Howard chimed in.

"Me too," Archie added. "But changing rivers slightly, Al, I want to go on record that I'm out because I don't have the workforce to look into this case right now. As you know, two of my staff and I are getting ready for Federal court for the next several weeks dealing with the confiscated shipment of criminal evidence and deciding what will be submitted during trial to best assist in proving our case. In addition, my investigative research analyst is working on something for the higher-ups, but I forgot what. Derrick is battling colon cancer, and Pete is still out with a broken leg and arm following his hiking accident."

Marino shook his head. "Wow!" he exclaimed, "you *are* out. However, I still need all of that in writing…today."

Archie smiled at Frank and Howard in an irritatingly smug way then bid them farewell and left Marino's office. Marino glanced at Frank again, then Howard.

"I want you two to work together on this. Howard, use Callahan. Frank, use Kelvin. He's the lowest 'hump' on your totem pole, right?"

Frank became blank, but only for a couple of seconds.

"Use Dennis Kelvin, our investigative research analyst?"

"Yes," Marino said in a brief but clearly effective manner. "At this juncture it's just a preliminary investigation which is usually conducted before opening a full investigation. Callahan is quite resourceful so Kelvin should learn a lot. If it becomes any more important, we'll bring in you big guns, okay? Once your investigation is complete, and if it warrants more than curiosity, we will then forward our findings to the US Attorney's Office. They can decide what's next."

Howard and Frank shook their heads as they were leaving Marino's office. Both knew Marino was just punishing them for not appearing at the New Agent Indoctrination.

***

Sandra Callahan and SA Dennis Kelvin took seats at the small square table in the building's cafeteria. Kelvin adjusted his clip-on tie and looked young enough to still suffer from acne. Since they had never met, both of their supervisors agreed they should connect and share thoughts on researching the charges made by the NALA representatives.

The idea was that when they met with their supervisors later, they could spew out the facts, and then it could be determined whether there was any merit to the allegations.

"I think we should interview Ms. Kincaid and Mr. Osman again, but separately," Callahan announced after sipping her coffee. "This way, we can make sure of any dent in their story and see how consistent they are with the details."

Kelvin agreed by bobbing his head. "To be honest, Callahan…"

"Sandra," she interjected.

"Sandra. I'm just a desk jockey. I can analyze, examine, survey, inspect, and conclude a problem on computer or paper, but interviewing, questioning, and answering folks one-on-one has not been part of my DNA here in this building."

"Dennis, listen up," she said, half smiling while flipping her red braid from one shoulder to the other, "we've been given this tiny little job that no one, I repeat, no one wants to do. We're going to do this job, and we're going to do it well. You got me?"

He nodded affirmatively while gulping his coffee.

***

The NALA office was within walking distance of the field office building. Although Callahan had heard the old saying so many times before that "visiting Washington, DC in the spring should be on everyone's bucket list," for some strange reason, today, she agreed. It had finally stopped raining, and the cherry blossoms were everywhere! Usually, she didn't give a rat's ass about them because, along with them *being* everywhere, so was the pollen, and so were the people sneezing in all directions.

"I guess when Japan gave us those few trees a century ago," she remarked to Kelvin, "I'm sure we didn't for one minute believe they would become this invasive."

"Still," he said with a smile, "Japan should feel a little envious because we can now boast that we have the most beautiful cherry blossom festival every single year."

He then stumbled on a crack in the sidewalk.

Callahan looked back at him. "Yeah, okay, whatever." She shook her head.

They reached the office of NALA, a four-story greystone, which, to Callahan, seemed void of any finery on its facade. The lobby proved the same. It made a lot of sense, according to Ms. Kincaid, that it "is more important what NALA does than how NALA looks." The receptionist directed them to the elevator and they got off on the fourth floor, where Georgia Kincaid was waiting for them and greeted them.

After displaying their identification, she shook both agent's hands while pointing toward an office.

"I don't know what else I can tell you that I didn't say in the meeting yesterday with your superiors," she said as she pointed toward a sofa in her office.

"First of all, thank you for seeing us, Ms. Kincaid," Callahan said sincerely. "As you know, we want to ensure we understand the landscape before barging into unknown territory. Trafficking of human beings is something all law enforcement takes seriously. We want to make sure we have concrete evidence of any labor trafficking before we knock down any doors."

After about an hour of conversation and realizing Kincaid had pretty much repeated what she had said in the meeting at FBI headquarters, Callahan felt as if she hadn't learned anything new. However, Kincaid was quite receptive to the idea that Mr. Osman *should also* be interviewed and would maybe provide further evidence of what they both believed was trafficking taking place. Ms. Kincaid made a call and within an hour both agents were granted permission by Amadi Osman to walk through his doors.

Baltimore, MD

The neighborhood where Mr. Osman resided seemed quiet, but it was late morning so that any children would be in school. He mentioned that he was usually at home between late morning and early afternoon when he would return to his bus to pick up the schoolchildren again. The house was relatively easy to spot as Mr. Osman had parked his yellow school bus in the driveway. Although modest in size, the salmon-colored house seemed nicely maintained. Someone had painted the sofa-like swing on the front porch to match the house's color. The lawn, too, was meticulous. A slim middle-age woman answered the door and introduced herself as Mr. Osman's mother. Amadi Osman soon appeared and beckoned them inside.

"Thank you for your assistance, Mr. Osman," Callahan began while flashing her FBI identification. "This is my partner Special Agent Kelvin. Why don't you tell us why you think children on your route are being led elsewhere and not into the programs for which you are dropping them off?"

Osman looked at his mother and signaled her into

another room.

"I do not want my parents involved," he said as he watched his mother leave the room. "Also, I would like to know if my name will in any way be mentioned in this scenario because if so, I will be terminated, and I cannot afford to be terminated as my siblings and I take care of our parents, ensuring that we are all safe."

Callahan looked puzzled. "Safe from what, or who, Mr. Osman?"

He took his time answering. "Mostly from the Kelsy-Wahauser Foundation, which supposedly runs the afterschool program in the building, but also from enemies of the Muslim Brotherhood who sometimes harass us."

He looked toward the door through which his mother exited.

"My father's youngest brother was an agrarian unionist in Sudan, who was seeking equal protection for all Sudanese, but especially protection from the Brotherhood, a group which committed widespread atrocities like arrest, torture, and execution of labor union officials and other civil society leaders. My twenty-two-year-old uncle was found dead in an alley with a garrote around his neck and a sign *stapled* to his stomach that read, 'The Brotherhood is alive and well. Watch your children.' We didn't need any further message. My parents, siblings, and I were on the next boat to the United States. We stayed for nine months in New York in a familial retreat, then moved here to Baltimore, where my family could continue tobacco farming."

Kelvin broke in. "Mr. Osman, you really think the Brotherhood, as you call them, is harassing you here in the US? You've been here almost two decades. You said yourself that employees of the Kelsy-Wahauser Foundation requested you to stop talking to the police. Could it not be them disguised as the Brotherhood?"

Callahan seemed impressed with his questions.

"Agent…" Osman began.

"Kelvin…Dennis Kelvin." He immediately showed him his ID…again.

Osman pointed to the kitchen table where they each sat down. "Agent Kelvin, I drop six children off at Kelsy-Wahauser Foundation Monday through Friday. It's a program where kids can go after regular school to do their homework, play in the yard, have a snack, and wait for their parents to pick them up or the other children wait for the Christian Orphanage to pick them up. Two weeks ago I felt something strange that day as I watched the kids enter the storefront building. I suddenly realized one of the kids had left their schoolbooks on one of the seats, so I went into the building but did not see the kids. I walked around the place but could not find any of the kids. I know that place holds about twenty-five kids, but I couldn't find them anywhere, and no adult was in sight."

"What do you mean no adult was in sight?" Callahan asked in a confusing tone.

"I mean, *no* adult was in sight. I left the schoolbooks on the front receptionist's desk and returned to my bus. As I drove away and passed the alley of the building, I saw the kids in the alley with two white men lifting white burlap-type bags of what looked like either flour or sugar into a gray van."

"How do you know what was in the bag Mr. Osman?" Callahan asked.

"I only know it looked like flour or sugar because a bag busted when it hit the ground. One of the white men slapped the little girl who dropped the bag. When the kids finished loading the van, it drove off. The same procedure happened the following week.”

Kelvin was writing everything down.

“Mr. Osman,” Callahan murmured in a somewhat hushed tone. “We will check out this sequence of events, and if we find improprieties like you feel you have witnessed, we will certainly follow up with a course of action.”

Osman escorted them to the door. Both agents strolled toward their nondescript vehicle with seemingly heavy thoughts on their minds.

FBI Washington Field Office, Washington, DC

The writing on the door read Supervisory Agent in Charge (SAC). Today, Frank was busy looking for answers, a task that made him feel less in charge than ever. Callahan and Kelvin were now in his face, but their findings were lacking, forcing Frank to focus on Callahan for any possible answers.

“What’s the nature of the labor-intensive work the children are being forced to do? Is it related to the afterschool program’s supposed activities or something entirely different?”

“At this time, Frank,” she said, “we have no answers. Basically we just followed up with Mr. Osman to further any inclination to delve into this matter.”

“How many children are affected, and what’s their age range?”

“There are six eight- to twelve-year-olds, sir,” Kelvin answered, with a slight quiver in his voice.

Frank looked at him. *Analysts.* "Who's leading the exploitation? Is it a group, or an organization? What's the motivation behind the exploitation? Is it human or labor trafficking, or both?"

"Wow, Frank," Callahan said shaking her head. We're just reporting preliminary findings. If you want more answers, let us find them."

"Okay, okay, but I'm making you lead on this, Callahan. I'll tell Howard when he returns from his so-called freedom weekend. Bring me facts, and we'll move on from there."

Callahan and Kelvin left Frank Leslie's office and connected in the hallway.

"Follow me to my office," she said to Kelvin. He followed her obediently.

Once inside her small but sunny office, she directed Kelvin to an empty chair in front of her customized desk, which she had brought with her from Quantico. Portraits of the President of the United States, J. Edgar Hoover, and the current FBI Director graced one wall. On her desk was a portrait of her granddad, Flynn Callahan.

"I just talked with a friend formerly in Homeland Security," she began. "He told me that labor trafficking is increasing and that he said he saw so many children put to work and found law enforcement officials so unwilling to investigate these cases that he felt forced to resign. He also said some of these kids Mr. Osman might be speaking about are far from home, and many are under intense pressure to earn money. They send cash back to their families while often being in debt to their sponsor's rent and living expenses. You're the analyst, tell me what we do next."

He looked at her without flinching. "Give me two days."

Alexandria, VA

The two-story pale-green house with the dark green shutters and circular drive was one of those Victorian types men would never pick out, but their wives love them. This house was no different. Sitting at the end of the cul de sac in the upscale neighborhood provided peace and quiet for its occupants except when they played basketball on the driveway.

Howard was out of breath. He sat on the antique-looking black wrought-iron loveseat on the grassy side of the driveway and watched as his thirteen-year-old twins, George and Lawrence, continued to shoot the basket above the garage doors. George called out to him. "Dad, are you coming back in?" Howard looked at him with the look that would have made a regular kid shrink, but not *his* kids, who ended up laughing way too long as far as Howard was concerned.

"C'mon, Dad," Lawrence pleaded. "You can't be that tired. We've only been playing an hour." With that unneeded piece of information, Howard got up from the loveseat, said adios to the boys, and limped into the house. Once inside, he limped swiftly to the ringing phone on the kitchen wall. It was his oldest son Mark who was in his last year of law school outside Chicago. All Howard could remember from the conversation was a bunch of yeses and the one no. *No, I did not forget that I am picking you up from Dulles tomorrow morning.*

Howard could not recall the last time that he and all three boys were going to be home together without their mom—an all-man weekend. And what made it even better was that Tim and Ahmad would be bringing their sons too, and the BBQ Men's Weekend was on!

Philadelphia, PA

Since quite a few women invitees were from outside the Philadelphia area, *all* invitees gathered downtown at the Philadelphia Marriott, where quite a few of them were staying, and enjoyed an evening of dinner and cocktails afterward. They would meet again at Janet's and Allen's house for the next day's baby shower. It was an eclectic group of women from Janet's childhood through college and current colleagues. The group also included Janet's mom, Juliana, and Allen's mom, Charlotte.

The chatter was nonstop but tremendous fun. Although the Knox's had invited the husbands and partners to the shower, all were unwilling to tread into *women's territory*.

Carol stood to speak.

"I'd like to make a toast," she said, holding her champagne glass. "Although they are not here, may Janet and Allen be blessed with patience, love, and wisdom as they embark on this wonderful journey called parenthood."

The women clinked their glasses together. At that moment, Allen's mom stood. Everyone waited for the pearls of wisdom.

"I thought Allen would never get married, much less have a child," she said with a smile wider than the Nile. She then sat down. The laughter was explosive.

***

When Allen Knox saw the mob of women showing up for the baby shower, he made Janet *promise* to not let on to any of the women, especially his mother, that he was in the house. He needed his sanity to be intact. He grabbed three beers from the fridge, a bag of Red Twizzlers and a bag of chips and salsa from the cabinet and ducked upstairs to their bedroom, planning never to be seen for the next three hours.

***

The music, laughter, screams, and the never-ending sounds of "ooh and ahh" went on for the next two hours. Then the doorbell rang, and Janet's mom went to answer it—a young man delivering a giant bouquet.

"Who is it, Mom?" Janet yelled.

"Flowers!" she yelled back.

The bouquet was too large for Juliana Forrestal to carry, so the young man carried them in and placed them on the dining room table as requested. His gray uniform showed Keller's Forest Flowers stitched on the shirt pocket. He looked back at the ladies as he was about to leave.

"All of you," he said as he exhibited a .38 Special, "have a seat. I'm going to need Carol Watson to step over here," as he pointed with his gun to a spot near the door.

All of the women were speechless. Janet put both hands on her stomach.

"What do you need Carol for?" she asked, almost stuttering.

"Don't worry about her," he said eerily calmly. "Worry about you and the other fine ladies here."

Carol looked perplexed. "What could I have possibly

done to you that you require a gun to get my attention?"

Charlotte Knox was about to faint. Several women rushed to her aid.

"Stay where you are—all of you!" he yelled. "Carol Watson will get her some water."

Carol then went to the dining table and poured a glass of water from the pitcher. She walked over to Charlotte and assisted her while she drank from the glass.

Janet grabbed her stomach again. "I need...I need to sit down," she said.

"Let her sit down!" Juliana yelled at the man.

He motioned Janet to sit at the table. CIA Officer Liling Xu and FBI Special Agent Katherine Perry remained quiet, knowing they had their weapons in their purses under the mattress in the next room.

"Ladies," he said with no cutting or biting tone, "I'm going to ask you all to have a seat. Although you might think I'm the villain in this scenario, I want you to know that the real villain here is Carol Watson."

Everyone looked at Carol, who looked just as confused as everyone else.

"Look, young man," Carol fired away, "I have no idea who you are or why you must feel you need a gun to make your point here. I want you to make that point before we call the police."

"Carol Watson, you're not going to call the police because I have enough bullets to stop you and anyone else who wants to become brave. Also, I have one for myself."

Juliana Forrestal rose from her seat to comfort her daughter, who clutched her eight-month-pregnant stomach.

"Sit back down," he said forcefully but not yelling.

Juliana glared at him. "Do what you want with me," she

said to him, "But I'm going over there, and I'm going to sit with my daughter."

He acknowledged her mama bear with a slight smile. Liling Xu and Kat Perry remained quiet but glanced at each other intermittently.

The man looked over at Carol. "Carol Watson, you don't know me, but you knew my father. Does the name Eric Glenn ring a bell?"

Carol took a moment before speaking. "You mean former FBI Special Agent Eric Glenn, who shot me fourteen years ago and left me for dead? That Eric Glenn?"

All eyes were on Joel Stover. "Yes, same Eric Glenn. I suppose you don't know that he was going to be released from prison tomorrow, but he took the easy way out and died of cancer instead."

"Well, I'm sorry about that," she said sincerely, "but what does this have to do with me?"

"If your husband hadn't sent my father to prison—"

"Your father sent himself to prison and—"

"Mrs. Watson, don't interrupt me again."

Carol became silent.

"As I said, your husband sent my father to prison based on *your* testimony. The FBI is at fault here, and I want to correct the outcome."

"What outcome?" Carol asked. "Don't tell me, like father like son?"

He began slowly, almost slurring his speech. "Your husband sending my father to prison caused a lot of misery. Our family became social outcasts, and my mother had to fight the FBI for months to secure my father's pension. We lost the case because my father's crimes were directly related to what the FBI conveniently called national security."

Joel blinked nervously and wiped his brow with his sleeve. He paused. "All because of you and your husband, Mrs. Watson…all because of you."

He made all the women place their cell phones on the floor. He then kicked them all to the side in a heap.

Carol looked around the room at the scared, hurt, and confused faces. "What do you want from me?" She asked almost apologetically.

"I want your husband to apologize for messing up my family's life."

Alexandria, VA

Seems the sun was trying to depart the earth as loudly as possible as it burst into flames when it hit the horizon. Howard, Mark, and Ahmad each stretched out on the backyard chaise lounges. Howard rubbed his stomach while downing the last ounces of his beer.

"The barbecue was delicious," Ahmad mentioned while sipping a glass of beer. "Too bad Tim had to leave. But if we're being honest, it can get exhausting having a two-year-old."

"Don't I remember," Howard said with a smirk.

Ahmad looked toward the house as he heard loud boy noises.

"I know they're all thirteen, Howard," Ahmad said with an equal smirk, "but I sure hope our boys don't kill your house. "Carol will come home, and you and Mark will be toast."

Mark looked up from his phone. "Why do you have to

bring me into this, Ahmad? Those are your and Dad's kids. Anyway, Dad, have you heard from Mom? How'd it go?"

Howard took a moment before putting down his drink. "I haven't, which is strange because I wanted to confirm picking her up at Dulles tomorrow at two p.m. so she could see you before your flight. You haven't heard from her?"

"No," Mark said, avoiding hoisting a flag. "It's strange, like you said, because between last night and this afternoon she must have called me five times to check on me and the boys, including you, Dad. But I haven't heard a peep from her since around three today. That was three hours ago. Something's not right."

"Yeah, that doesn't sound like your mother. Hold on, let me call her."

Howard dialed Carol's phone and received a voice message. He left a message.

"They probably all ran out of juice taking so many pictures on their phones. So their phones are all probably charging."

Mark then called his mother and also had to leave a message.

"Why don't you call Knox, Howard?" Ahmad asked.

"Right, Ahmad, let's see what's up."

***

The absence of noise downstairs for the past ten minutes piqued Knox's curiosity. *Did something happen? Should I really venture into no-man's land?* These thoughts and the basketball game ran across his brain simultaneously. He believed if he went downstairs, he would never return. He knew what his mother and Janet's mother looked like, so there was no one downstairs that he needed to see more than the game. Besides, his team was kicking butt. He decided to wait until halftime.

***

It was halftime. Knox was moving slowly down the back carpeted stairs to avoid being noticed on his way to the kitchen when he heard a man's voice. At first, he thought the television was on until he heard Juliana screaming that she was going to sit with her daughter.

Knox then crept closer to the wall to listen to more. He realized quickly that Carol and possibly the rest of the women, especially his very pregnant wife Janet, were in trouble. He tried listening to more conversations. He sensed the man talking was young. Knox crept back upstairs. Although Liling Xu and Kat Perry were guests at the shower, he surmised that their weapons were safely in another room. His phone started vibrating—it was Howard. He had to think quickly.

14 years ago –

John Mason was in his car and on his way home. He didn't know why, but he was suddenly struck with the memory of his friend Carl Sunderland's funeral. Carl's ex-wife, Joan, although divorced from Carl for three years, had been distraught. John remembered holding her hand throughout the service. He was relieved when it was finally over. John noticed through the car window that it was starting to rain. He was driving on a somewhat deserted stretch of highway and the darkness of the electrical storm and the hard rain bothered him. He squinted. As he turned on the car radio just checking for a weather report he noticed up ahead a green van pulling out into the intersection and then...stopping! John pressed his hand on the car horn and didn't let up. He put his foot on the brake...it didn't work! He bit his bottom lip. He swerved to avoid colliding with the van but ran off the shoulder of the highway and down a steep embankment. His car turned over twice, breaking John's neck and killing him instantly. The green van waited a moment, and then drove off.

Carol Mason glanced down at her son at her husband's funeral and wondered how she could possibly live without her husband. John had been a good husband and a great father. He was an FBI agent who had died in a car accident. She couldn't believe that her husband was dead! He was only thirty-seven years old. He had a lot of life to live. She kept telling herself that he hadn't died in vain. There had to be an outside cause for his death and she was going to find it! Carol knew in her heart that John had been murdered, and by someone he knew. She would not stop until she found out by whom and why. His colleagues had assured her that the "Bureau" would investigate the accident; she somehow suspected everyone, but she didn't know why.

John Mason had been an FBI agent for over ten years. He used to tell her and Mark that there were elements relating to his line of work that he couldn't discuss with them. It was part of his job not to discuss. "You don't need to know them anyway, Carol," he would say. He had been working on a case that had consumed his last thirty days. He hadn't been himself. He had been abnormally preoccupied. He was working on something that had completely overtaken him. He wasn't talkative any longer, and he wasn't John any longer.

After John's funeral, Carol and Mark moved from Chicago to Washington, DC where Carol's mother and three brothers still resided. Carol felt that she and Mark could start over in a different city. She would return to teaching and Mark would receive a well-rounded education in the nation's capital. Most of all, she knew she couldn't stay in the same city where her husband had been killed. John had mentioned to Carol on several instances that if anything were to happen to him, she and Mark were to go to Washington, DC where they would be safe. They would have to locate an agent named Howard Watson. He said they could surely trust Howard.

Washington, DC

The Kronen Group found its footing in 1939 in Washington, DC, with the help of James Butler-Kronen, an accountant from a very well-to-do family who was probably its only member who believed in the working class. Despite his family's financial achievements, James believed in the power of practical skills and the importance of those who kept society running. He saw a world that needed people to ensure the lights stayed on, the water flowed, and infrastructure was maintained. After being left a hefty sum in his grandfather's will, Butler-Kronen, at age thirty-six, purchased a six-bedroom, three-story greystone mansion. A year later, with his wife's approval, he quit his job and turned the mansion into a six-office establishment designed to handle all the paperwork and payroll for four tobacco manufacturing concerns in Maryland.

Within a decade, The Kronen Group had expanded into four five-story buildings, symbolizing its rapid growth. In just fifteen years, the company's workforce had multiplied from thirty to over 1,200, operating with forty offices. The company's consistent recognition as a "Forbes 100 Great Places To Work" for over a decade was a testament to its focus on company morale, generous funding for underserved communities, and its foundation's commitment to transforming ignored land into thriving communities. It was always an easy choice for Forbes.

The executive wing of the company, a hub of strategic decision-making, was perched on the fifth floor of the main building. It housed eight executive offices, including the company's current CEO, Mitchell Butler-Kronen, who was nervously pacing the rich carpeted floor, a cigarette dangling in one hand and a glass of Jack Daniels on the rocks in the other.

James Butler-Kronen was a staunch advocate for the working class. His legacy, however, seemed to fade with each passing generation. The current Butler-Kronen cared about the working class only if they didn't show up for work.

Mitchell Butler-Kronen had only inherited the CEO position two years prior from his father, James Butler-Kronen, Jr., who became disabled after a car accident in which he lost a leg. James, Jr. tried to keep Mitchell in line while Mitchell worked his way up through the ranks of the Kronen Group. James, Jr. even made sure to refrain from naming Mitchell a James III so Mitchell could be who he would be. James, Jr. realized too late that Mitchell was a rogue Butler-Kronen.

James, Jr. desperately wanted to remain in the

Company's decision-making sanctum but the board, especially his son Mitchell, but including his wife, had driven him out, citing "health issues" that might get in the way. James, Jr. told a confidante he was furious in the way they ousted him; he hoped he was dead before Mitchell took the company down. He believed his father was turning over in his grave.

***

Butler-Kronen's office not only housed his oversized mahogany desk but also a sofa, cocktail table, and conference table that could accommodate six chairs. His large picture window looked out onto the Potomac River, and he could usually be caught standing in front of it for more than a minute as he was doing when his VPs arrived. Butler-Kronen had called a meeting in his office with his Executive VP and two VPs to discuss the whistleblower "situation." Each man took a seat at the conference table. Butler-Kronen sat at one end.

"I don't care what it takes to get rid of this little roach," he told the three men, "I want this nobody bus driver gone.

"What exactly do you mean by 'gone,' Mitch?" the EVP asked.

"Let him lose his job, an eye, or a limb if that will get him off our scent. We are doing profitable business with those kids working for our clients; no one is complaining except this bus driver. Threaten his parents…does he have a wife or kids?"

Another man answered. "No, Mitch, we don't believe he's married nor has any children. He lives with his parents."

"Then send a note to the parents to cease talking to law

42

enforcement about what he thinks he has seen. Am I clear?"

***

Amadi Osman had been missing for twenty-four hours when Mrs. Osman received a phone call from an unknown caller who told her that if she wanted her son returned alive, she and her husband should convince him how crucial it is to him *and them* to make the authorities believe what he reported was all a mistake.

Instead of being afraid of the phone call, Mrs. Osman was adamant about seeking justice once Amadi was safely returned. "I'll be damned if we let these demonic beings try to destroy our lives," she told her husband. "They have shown us their hand."

Mr. Osman looked her straight in the eyes. "Once Amadi is safely returned, we fight. We fight to finish. Isn't that what we promised each other, Aamira?"

Mrs. Osman angrily smiled. "Yes, Abdo, this little nothing group has come up on a real threat—us Sudanese—who already know what hell looks like."

She then called the FBI headquarters to speak to Sandra Callahan. The operator told her that Agent Callahan was not in the office because it was Saturday but would return on Monday. She was also told, "If the call is urgent, someone from her office will return the call within an hour."

Mrs. Osman thanked the operator and said she would wait for Agent Callahan to return her call. She made the call to record that at least she called before she and her family sought Plan B.

***

"What?" Howard's voice trembled with disbelief. "What?!!" His words echoed with a mix of shock and concern.

As Knox explained what he thought was going on downstairs, he also mentioned the overwhelming precariousness of the situation—mainly his pregnant wife. Ahmad and Mark's eyes widened, their glances filled with a potent mix of fear and curiosity. The moment was heavy with unspoken questions, and like a hidden secret, the truth remained beyond their grasp.

"Okay, okay, Knox," Howard said on the phone. "I'm on the next plane. Get in touch with Stanton Abrams, Philly Office, now. And make sure Xu and Perry don't try to be heroes."

"Howard, I have to get in touch with my boss, too," Knox said. "McIlvane is gonna have a stroke knowing I called the FBI first. I don't know who the man is, but he seems to have some sort of grievance with your wife."

"What do you mean, Knox…with my wife?"

"I mean, he has singled her out for some strange reason I can't explain. He keeps mentioning that whatever the problem is it's her fault."

The talk ceased for a pregnant moment. Finally, Howard looked at Mark and Ahmad before choosing his words.

"Knox, I know you, and this will require a lot of patience but that's what you're built for. From what you've heard, this situation seems personal, so I need to know who that man is."

"Okay, Howard, but I'm telling you right now if—"

"I'm with you, Knox, but let's not go there yet. I'll be there in seventy minutes. You gotta hang on."

Howard hung up but took his time looking at Mark.

"What is it, Dad?" Mark shouted. "What's wrong?"

"Mark, I need you to stay an extra day to watch your brothers."

Chevy Chase, MD

Chevy Chase, a town located just outside Washington, DC, was primarily residential. It boasted a famous shopping district and was the home of several private country clubs whose members included many prominent politicians and Washingtonians. For decades, Chevy Chase was known as the "most educated town in America," with over ninety percent of its adult residents having at least a bachelor's degree. Most houses had two- and three-car garages.

Alberto Marino resided in one of these houses. He was sitting on his back patio steps, wiping his forehead with a handkerchief and glancing at his now-mowed lawn. Marino smiled a simple smile that only came with the pleasure of doing something worthwhile. He loved anything that had to do with maintaining the outside of his house. Today it was mowing the lawn. His calm was quickly interrupted when he answered his cell phone.

"It's Saturday, Howard, make it quick."

"What?!!" Marino's voice thundered through the phone, his disbelief and anger concrete. He stood up and started pacing. "Who the hell is this guy?"

"At this time, I don't know, Al," Howard said as calmly as he could, as not to giveaway to Marino that he wanted to get to Philly and kill the sonofabitch holding his wife. However, what came out of his mouth was: "But he is holding twenty women hostage, including my wife and Forrestal, for some reason we can't explain at this time."

Howard too started pacing while talking to Marino. "I need to get to Philly now, Al."

"Sure, sure, Howard, but does Carol or Forrestal even know this guy?"

"Don't know, Al, but if anything happens to—"

"Nothing will happen to Carol, Forrestal, or any of those women, Howard. I'll..."

Howard blew out a breath. "Al, Kelly Yamamoto, Liling Xu, and Philly Agent Kat Perry are also guests at the shower. I haven't told Tim yet."

Marino sat down on the stairs again. "Oh God. Who isn't at this shower? I'm calling Bruce now and…"

"…Knox has already called Stanton. He also called McIlvane, because Xu is at the shower."

"I'm still calling Bruce, Howard. We don't want the CIA anymore in this situation as they have to be. Just so you know, I'm obligated to call the Hostage Rescue Team at Quantico and Philly SWAT.

"Al, too many weapons at this time and we don't really know about the guy and his intentions.

"Howard, the car is on its way. Call me when you get on the chopper."

"Of course, Al."

✳✳✳

Knox paced back and forth in the bedroom, trying to devise a solution that would not let the man know that he was law enforcement. He strapped his personal Glock to his ankle, put his fake phone in his back pocket, put his real phone on vibrate, and placed it inside his thigh. Then, he ventured down the back stairs again and out the back door.

✳✳✳

Amadi Osman was "dropped" off on an empty street at eleven p.m. He walked the four blocks to his school bus, which was still parked in front of the Yorkshire building. Except for the swollen lip, black eye, broken tooth, and possibly a broken wrist, Amadi was alive. He drove home slowly, with his good hand on the wheel, to his parents and brother waiting for him in his driveway. After parking the bus and taking a bathroom break, he sat patiently on a barstool while his mother wrapped his now swollen wrist with gauze and nursed his eye and lips with a handkerchief filled with ice cubes. Afterward, his brother drove him to the nearest hospital. Amadi sat in the front seat, and his father sat in the backseat.

"Do you know who did this to you, Amadi?" his father asked, almost with an eerie calmness.

"No, Father, I do not," he answered, holding his limp wrist. "However, I do know who is responsible."

"Who, Amadi, who?" his brother asked nervously.

"It is the Foundation or the Kronen Group Ibrahim."

"Why do you know this to be true?" his father asked, now obviously angered.

Wincing slightly in pain, Amadi turned around slowly in his seat to face his father.

"Because one of the three men told me to 'shut your mouth about the foundation or we will shut it for you.'"

Amadi's father grinned slightly and shook his head. "You know, of course, Amadi, I must ask you this one question. Do you want to keep your job?"

"Yes, Father, I do. I will be finished with graduate studies in a few months, and this position pays well. The hours work especially well for me, and I really care about the children."

"Then we will not kill your enemy. But we will make those who caused you this physical harm pay for your loyalty to the children."

Amadi turned back around in his seat. He looked over at his brother, who was nodding to his father's words.

Georgetown neighborhood, Washington, DC

Georgetown, a historic neighborhood and commercial district in Washington, DC, lay along the Potomac River. It was a vibrant and diverse community, home to a mix of politicians, lobbyists, and various specialty retailers and fashionable boutiques. The western edge of Georgetown housed not only the main campus of Georgetown University but chic three-story townhouses, greystone and brownstone mansions, and upscale single housing. Tim Yamamoto, his wife, Kelly, and their two-year-old son, Timmy, were part of this diverse community, residing in one of these chic townhouses.

Tim had just rocked Timmy to sleep when Howard rang his doorbell. With a sense of anticipation, he thought it peculiar that Howard had to see him *after* the BBQ because he could have said anything to him in front of Ahmad. He bounded down the stairs before Howard rang the bell again and woke the baby.

"What?" was all that came out of Tim's mouth. He started pacing back and forth in his kitchen.

As much as Howard tried explaining that he, Knox, and the Philly Office would take care of the person wreaking havoc on the group of women at the shower, he could not convince Tim to stay put.

"Howard…" Tim's voice quivered. "It's not just a matter of a maniac on the loose. It's my wife, Howard. She's in danger, too."

"I know, Tim, and I hear you, but you're gonna have to stand down. We already have too many emotions flying, especially with Forrestal, who might go into pre-labor on this…and Knox, if we don't catch him in time, might be up for manslaughter charges."

"Howard," Tim began.

"Tim, listen to me. There's only one reason Al is allowing *me* to go to Philly and that's because this person, whoever he is, has singled out Carol. My wife. The mother of my children."

He paused. "You have a two-year-old son who needs you right now. You take care of little Tim, and I'll see to it that Knox and I take care of Kelly. You have my word. In the meantime, I'm hoping you can find out who this person is and what he has to do with my wife. Can you handle this?"

Tim blew out air. "Yeah, Howard. I can handle this."

***

Joel Stover was sent into a perplexing spin when most of the women had to go to the bathroom almost simultaneously. After nervously pacing back and forth, he signaled to Carol

Watson to follow him through the house. She motioned to the scared and mostly confused women to *don't do anything that might send him off.* So they all sat frozen at the dining room table. The guest bathroom was easily found on the first floor. After Joel noticed that there was no window large enough for a human to exit, he allowed the women to go to the toilet in twos. Once six rounds of women had their needs addressed, Xu and Perry were then allowed to go.

While Xu was in the bathroom, Perry slipped into the adjacent bedroom and rifled under the mattress to find their purses and guns. She slipped back into the bathroom, and she and Xu stuck their weapons inside the back of their pants. They walked back into the room to hear Forrestal crying for help.

"Mom, help me!" Forrestal cried out. As she grabbed her stomach with both hands, she bent over in the chair, wincing in pain.

Juliana yelled at Joel Stover. "We need a doctor! I think you've sent my daughter into an early labor!"

***

As Brett Hamilton and Kevin Lee were leaving the tennis court, their victory still fresh in their minds, Brett's phone vibrated. It was Tim. Tossing his gym bag into the car, Brett answered the call, his voice filled with anticipation.

"You must have heard that Kevin and I whupped butt, right?"

He paused. He then asked Tim to repeat the info dispensed to him to ensure he heard him correctly.

"I'll get on it right now, Tim." Brett's voice was tense with urgency. "Yes, he's right here with me. I'll tell him.

Okay, we're on it."

After revealing to Kevin the situation in Philadelphia, they jumped in the car. They headed to the FBI Headquarters to go through databases to hopefully gain some knowledge as to who this man might be.

They arrived at FBI Headquarters but because it was Saturday evening, the regular Monday-Friday security crew was not working, so the weekend crew, who did not believe their identification cards were sufficient, required each man's fingerprint on the glass button and their face in front of the camera. Once the computer verified their credentials, they took the specific elevator to the second floor. They had to use their facial recognition again to gain entrance to the library. Both men worked in different cubicles to do their research.

***

Knox had sprinted two blocks away from his home when he called his boss, Greg McIlvane, CIA, and his wife's boss, Stanton Abrams, FBI. He left messages for both on their cellphones. Stanton was the first to call back.

"Knox, I take it you haven't called Philly Police?"

"No Stanton, I don't want them in on this."

"Okay, but you're gonna have to step out of this because it's personal for you and its FBI territory. Do you hear me?"

Silence.

"Knox, do you hear me?"

"Yeah, Stanton, I hear you. But you really don't believe I'm gonna do nothing, do you?"

"Yes, I do, Knox, especially if you let us do our job. This is what we do, Knox, but you gotta let us do our job. Give me the specifics—the address—and what's around your house—a vacant lot, pond, a swimming pool? Are you sure it's just one individual?"

"I'm sending you the location via GPS. Yes, I heard only one male voice, so I'm fairly certain it's just one individual."

Pause.

"Just so you know, Stanton, Kat Perry is also at the shower."

"I figured. Knox, I know this is beneath you, but can you refrain from returning to your house until we get this under control?"

"Honestly, Stanton, I don't think I can do that."

"You know you can possibly hurt Forrestal's chances and that of your unborn child if you don't stand back and let us at least attempt to do our job. You have to trust us. Do you understand me...clearly?"

"Yes, Stanton, but I need you to stay with me every step of the way. You got that?"

He looked at his phone. "Stanton, I got McIlvane on my other line. He'll need to talk with you."

***

Shari Stover called her son several times but got no answer. She then called her daughter to see if she had heard from him. She hadn't. Shari couldn't read Joel as to how he really felt about his father not only dying, but dying in prison. She knew therapy had helped Gina emerge from her bulimia battle, but she didn't think it had helped Joel emerge from his inner demons.

Joel was a brilliant student, good-looking, and talented at not saying a word, even if he knew the word. It took therapists and Shari several years for Joel to come out of his corner and into the light. When he joined the chess team in high school, Shari thought perhaps he was showing signs of living. When he was accepted at University of Virginia, the only school he applied to, she smiled broadly. When he got his first job at a prestigious accounting firm, she exhaled. But with the news of his father's death, Shari saw sunlight leave Joel's face. After questioning him several times about his feelings, all he did was shrug and say, "I'm sorry, Mom, but his death, just like his life, means nothing to me."

Shari wasn't sure he was telling her the truth. Gina, on the other hand, was too young to know their father fully, and after moving the children away from the DC area, Shari was sure their father's absence would not upset their life. She was wrong. She quickly learned the stories people tell behind your back eventually slap you in the face.

As a teenager, Gina had heard many stories about her father and couldn't discern what was the truth. She felt perhaps she should have been a more doting daughter, and maybe he wouldn't have gone to prison. Her mother told her "rubbish." Gina started refusing food and then curiously eating a lot of food but throwing it up in the bathroom. When Shari, the nurse, became aware of Gina's weight loss and Shari, the mother, started seeing slips in Gina's grades at school, she immediately enrolled her in therapy. It only took two years for her to become whole again. By this time, Joel had slipped through her fingers.

She tried calling him again. *It's Saturday, Joel. Where are you?*

14 years ago –
Carol and Mark arrived at the Greyhound bus station

early enough to catch their six a.m. bus.

While traveling through Gary, Indiana, Carol's eyes moved about the bus. She was overwhelmed with anxiety. She glanced nonchalantly to the back of the bus and was surprised to see two well-dressed men pretending not to look at her. One was David Snell, an FBI agent who had been a close friend of her husband. She decided not to strike up a conversation with them unless they approached her, as she didn't want to do anything out of the ordinary or make herself obvious. She concluded that the Bureau had dispatched two agents to guarantee their safety to DC. She felt somewhat relieved. She took a quick peek at Mark, who was asleep. She then felt secure enough to close her eyes. She thought about absolutely nothing for a full moment then drifted into a needed sleep.

Arlington, VA

Across the Potomac from Washington, DC, Dennis Kelvin sat on his back porch with several male colleagues, watching the end of a closely matched basketball game. The whooping and yelling drowned out the two phone calls he missed twice. He answered on the caller's third try. It was Callahan.

"Yeah, Sandra," he answered.

"Dennis, I realize it's Saturday," she began.

The guys were still whooping it up.

"Sorry Sandra, I just saw that you have called…" He turned to his buddies with a finger on his lips to request silence.

"Three times," she said adamantly. "Do you have a report for Frank? If so, can I go over it before we present it?"

"Sure. I can send it email or text…what do you prefer?"

"Send it text."

The background voices were yelling excitedly.

"Have fun, Dennis…but send it tonight."

Callahan put her phone down on the table. She was sitting outside a cafe in the almost perfect late spring air, sipping a glass of white wine. Whistling and cawing from different birds caught her attention and made her smile. The slight breeze made the evening seem almost perfect. When her two girlfriends arrived, the waitress handed them menus and darted back inside the cafe.

"Well, ladies," she began, "I suggest starting with the bruschetta." She glanced at her phone. It was Tim. "Yes, sir, what can I do for you on this fine Saturday evening?"

***

Katherine Perry was not a member of the FBI SWAT Team, although she had expressed interest in SWAT selection. Still, she was well equipped with over three years of experience in the military in marksmanship, decision-making, leadership, and performing at her highest capacity for extended periods without rest. She recognized she was chosen for the FBI because of her previous military involvement and her background in combatting terrorist operations and providing medical assistance to injured members of the public and her team. In addition, she was an International Morse Code Translator and fluent in Spanish and Italian.

When she retrieved her and Xu's weapons from the

bedroom, she told no one that she had seen Allen Knox slip out the back door. She now recognized that the FBI would be entering the fray and deem this a hostage rescue with a barricaded suspect. She also recognized that a too-eager *municipal* SWAT team would not allow this young man to state his case and live to see another day.

Gregory McIlvane and Bruce Jergensen, Stanton Abrams' boss, discussed over the phone the need for drones.

"You should use local SWAT, Bruce," McIlvane said. "They know their streets best and can handle high-risk situations. They can also deploy their hostage rescue unit *and* you will agree with me that this is an extraordinary hostage situation. It's only right that you get local involved first. Also, probably most importantly, we have to prevent CIA Officer Allen Knox from making this guy a casualty before we know his story."

***

All the women, except perhaps Perry and Xu, were confused, tired, and scared. Carol sensed this in everyone. She believed it was up to her to diffuse the situation.

"Young man," she began. "Since I already know your father's name, what is your name?"

Just as Stover was about to answer Janet got up to go to the bathroom…again. As she stood up she felt a tightness in her body that made her groan loudly. "I think I'm in labor!" she shouted. Juliana helped her to the bathroom. Stover watched. Juliana returned only a few minutes later and announced with a concerned look at Stover. "Maybe."

Joel looked at her and then, hearing something outside the house, walked swiftly to a window, his gun still pointing to Carol, and peered out. He saw nothing.

He heard something again. This time, it was someone walking through the front door—Allen Knox. Joel turned his gun quickly to Knox. "Who…who are you?" he stammered.

Knox looked briefly at a surprised Janet who was walking out of the bathroom. He then glanced at Joel Stover's gun. "What the f…" he began. "Never mind who I am. That's my wife. What's with the gun? Who are you?"

A few women in the room started crying and stammering.

"All right," Joel yelled. "Everybody be quiet." He pointed to Knox. "Get over there with your wife, and don't make matters worse."

"Worse than what?" Knox yelled.

At that moment, Forrestal grabbed her stomach and winced in pain. Knox rushed to her side as Juliana yelled.

"Why don't you let her go to the hospital!!? Are you some kind of monster?"

"Yes, Joel!" Carol screamed. "Why don't you let all these women go? Your problem seems to be with me."

Knox glanced at Xu, then Perry. He gave them each the look of *I'll handle this*. However, he forgot he was dealing with two alpha females who were on the ready.

"What is this all about?" Knox remarked. "Why do you have a gun on these women? What the hell are you doing here? Again, who are you?"

"Mister whatever your name is, place your phone on the floor with the others. I suggest you sit next to your wife while Mrs. Watson phones her husband to meet us here."

Forrestal grabbed her stomach with both hands and winced in pain again. Juliana got up from her seat and walked toward Joel with the look of *I am going to kill you.*

Knox pulled her back.

"Ma'am, please don't," Joel yelled. "I didn't come here to hurt anyone, however, I now know that I will not live to see tomorrow so I suggest you retake your seat because I will use my gun."

Anacostia Neighborhood, Washington, DC

Anacostia, an historic community in Southeast Washington, DC, holds a significant place in history, with ties to one of the most prominent African Americans: Frederick Douglass. His home, a registered national historic site, is a testament to the neighborhood's rich past. The area's natural beauty, with its waterfront, wildlife, lotuses, water lilies, and walking trails, added charm. The well-kept lawns and houses reflected the residents' pride and respect for their community. Anacostia, designed to be affordable for Washington's working class, was now home to the Osman's daughter Amina and her husband Faheem Yousif. Their two-story house, painted a muted blue, with dark blue shutters, sat on the corner of a quiet block. The sofa-like swing on the wide front porch was painted the same color as the house.

Abdo, Aamira, Ibrahim, and Amadi were gathered at the dining room table. Faheem and Amina were standing, Faheem with his arm around Amina's waist. Abdo stood up to speak but the knock on the front door caused him to pause.

"Faheem," he said almost casually, "please allow our friends to join us."

Two very dark-skin muscular men bobbed their heads

quickly in Abdo's direction as they walked into the dining room and were shown two empty seats at the table. Abdo began.

"We must take care of Amadi's enemies. However, in this undertaking, the complications present themselves as incarceration or deportation if caught. I pray with God's assistance that it will not come to this. We do not back down. Our son, your brother, must finish his graduate studies. He must remain with his job, and most importantly, we do not and cannot condone the abuse of children anywhere. My brother, all praise be to God, did not die for nothing. He died for something."

"What are you asking of us, Father?" Amina asked.

"I am asking us to make a plan." He paused. "Faheem, Amadi is not your blood, and we are uncomfortable asking you to be part of our plan."

Faheem took his arm from around Amina's waist. "Abdo, when I married Amina, Amadi became my blood. I look at the beating he was given because he was protecting children. Children. I cannot condone this cowardly behavior at all. I will do whatever it takes to bring down the devil."

Amina smiled. As did the rest of the assemblage.

However, Abdo was adamant and shook his head. "Faheem, if you join us, you might have to forego your calligraphy and photography business for a while and Amina would have to stop teaching. We would owe you two a tremendous debt."

Everyone looked at Faheem.

"Abdo, you and Aamira moved the family thousands of miles away from your home for everyone's safety. You felt no alternative but to relinquish your tobacco business, and Aamira halted her weaving and pottery business. I say we owe you."

Throughout the one-hour meeting, the muscular men never spoke, but they seemed to listen carefully and clearly.

***

Brett Hamilton and Kevin Lee scanned every available database regarding Howard and Carol Watson's lives. Two hours in, Kevin whistled slightly. Brett was three cubicles over but still heard the whistle. Others in the library looked up from whatever they were doing when they heard the whistle.

"You find something, Kevin?" he whispered loudly.

"Think so. Come here and tell me if you agree."

Brett closed down the computer he was using and strolled over to Kevin's cubicle. Kevin pointed to two articles fourteen years apart.

"Wow!" was all that Brett could muster up to say.

"I'll call Al."

***

Howard Watson jumped off the Airbus Helicopter at Philadelphia International Airport, and Special Agent Gil Holloway was there to greet him. They shook hands as they ran to the waiting black SUV.

"Got some news for you, Howard," he began.

They got into the car, and Holloway's boss, Stanton Abrams, was already inside.

"Not the greatest way to get together," Abrams started. "How you doin', Howard?"

"I've been better, Stanton," he answered as they shook

hands.

"Bruce just sent me this information from Al. Look at these two articles. Tell me what you think."

Howard glanced at the first article and then the second. "So the first is about David Snell and Eric Glenn going to prison. The second is about Eric Glenn's death?"

"Yes," Abrams answered.

Howard took a moment. "Stanton, you think the man is related to Snell or Glenn?"

"Yes, we do," Abrams replied. "Which is why your CIA pal said he heard the perp single out your wife. We're betting the man is Eric Glenn's son."

Howard blew out a breath and then called Marino.

"Yeah, Howard," Marino said on the phone. "Our guys scanned the archives. We are now looking at the Glenn family, who seem to have disappeared about thirteen years ago. Maybe they've changed their name, moved, I dunno. I recall the wife, Shari, I believe was her name, took a lot of flak from the DC community. Call me when you get to Stanton's office, and I will update any information."

"Al," Howard began.

"No, Howard, do not attempt any heroics, just like you would tell your team. It seems this young man, who is probably twenty-four, twenty-five, at the most, has been holding the women hostage for over four hours now, so he doesn't seem to be in a hurry to do whatever he is or was planning."

14 years ago –

Carl Sunderland was frantic. The speedometer read 90 mph, then 95. When it reached 100, he decided to slow down. "No sense in killing myself before I reach FBI Headquarters," he muttered. He noticed a green van following him. After many miles, he finally acted on the suspicion that he was being followed. He pulled into the 7-Eleven store parking lot to use the phone. He called the number on the card. It was an FBI agent named John Mason.

"I have urgent information for Mason and only Mason," he told the secretary.

"Mr. Mason is still on vacation, like I told you yesterday, sir," she said. "He won't be back until Monday."

Since this was Thursday, Sunderland left a phone number and hung up. When he returned to his car, he noticed that the green van following him was nowhere to be seen. Sunderland felt uneasy but drove off, his tires screeching. Minutes later, he heard a faint hissing sound coming from the back seat, so he pulled over to the shoulder of the road. As he turned his head to check on the sound, his car exploded, throwing him through the front window, killing him instantly.

FBI Philadelphia Field Office, Philadelphia, PA

Howard called Knox to let him know he was in Philadelphia. Although he got a voice message, it indicated to Howard that Knox's phone was on vibrate, but he probably saw that he called. Howard could wait because, right now, he was at Stanton's office outlining a plan. Stanton was seated at his desk, and Howard sat in one of the two empty chairs facing Stanton's desk. Bruce Jergensen, Stanton's boss, walked into the room and shook Howard's hand before sitting at Stanton's small conference table.

"Howard, good to see you, but not for this reason."

"Ditto, Bruce," he answered.

"What does the landscape look like, guys?" he asked.

Both men seemed reluctant to speak, especially since neither had more information than Bruce; however, it was Stanton's call. "We're just waiting for confirmation on the Glenn family's whereabouts, especially young Glenn's background."

Jergensen got up from the table, walked over to Stanton's window, and looked at the greenery and traffic. He was still facing the window when he sighed. "What is our world coming to?"

Before anyone could answer, Stanton's EA was on his desk speakerphone. "Stanton, is Director Jergensen still in with you and Howard Watson?"

"Yes, Katie," he answered. Why?"

"I have Director Marino on the line, hoping he could catch all of you together."

"Okay, put him through."

Jergensen took the other empty chair facing Stanton's desk. "Yeah, Al," Jergensen began. "What do you have?"

"Seems our boys here did some digging on young Glenn's background. The mother, Shari, changed their surname to her maiden name—Stover—about thirteen years ago. The son, Joel Stover, works at Carlton & Associates accounting firm in your neck of the woods, Bruce."

"I know that firm well, as several team members worked there. What else can you tell us?"

"Well, I have Kevin Lee, one of Howard's people, here who can give you the rest of this story."

The next thing they heard was the rustling of papers, Jergensen looking slightly annoyed, and finally, Lee's voice.

"This is Agent Lee…"

"We know who you are, Lee," Stanton quipped. Howard was not smiling.

"Sir, fourteen years ago, Chicago Special Agent David Snell was found guilty of a criminal attempt to commit a felony, which was kidnapping through false pretenses of Carol Mason and her then ten-year-old son Mark Mason. Snell hadn't served three months when he met his demise in Elkton, Ohio Federal Prison. His partner in this scheme, another Chicago Special Agent, Eric Glenn, was convicted of the same crime but it also included assault with a deadly weapon for which he had discharged his weapon and critically wounded Carol Mason, now Carol Watson. Before entering prison, Glenn was the father of a ten-year-old son, Joel, who is now twenty-four, and a six-year-old daughter, Gina, who is now twenty and a junior at Temple University. Their mother, Shari, currently a Nurse Practitioner at Penn Medicine, moved with the children, from DC to Philadelphia to protect them, we believe, from the relentless pressure of the media."

Stanton begged the question. "Lee, do you believe the mother and the sister know that Joel is capable of what he is preparing to go to jail for?"

"I would say no, sir, simply because after interviewing Stover's boss and secretary, both seem thoroughly rattled by the idea that this young man can cause harm to anyone. Both believe we have the wrong person. Which we do not, sir."

Marino came back on speaker. "Bruce, you gotta get the mother and sister in. They will have to diffuse this situation because the CIA has informed us that their Officer Knox is now in the house with the perp."

"What!?" Howard exclaimed. "What!?"

14 years ago –

Carol wondered why they had to get to Howard Watson and why he didn't even attend John's funeral. She recalled how many times John had written about him in his letters from the army. How many times did he mention Howard and their Academy days? How many times did Howard apologize over and over again for not making it to their wedding because he was on assignment in a remote part of Colombia? She had never met him but knew Howard was important to John's life.

But WHERE WAS HE? She had sent him a telegram and left a detailed message with his service regarding John's death and subsequent funeral. But no Howard! Finally, after several calls to his home, she called the FBI Headquarters in Washington, DC, and was informed that he was on assignment out of the country. Carol felt this was a bad omen.

The "Bureau" said that John had died in a car accident. His brakes had gone out. Carol knew that it was too coincidental. What was John working on that took his life?

Carol and Mark decided to take a bus to DC. After stopping in Indianapolis and buying various sundries, they were walking back toward their bus when two FBI agents approached them. One of them, David, had been a colleague of her husband, John. David said he had to talk to her. He said it was a matter of life and death. Fear ran through her body, and the blood in her veins froze. She tried to be calm but couldn't help blurting out, "David, what is happening to us?"

He grabbed her shaking body and tried to calm her down. "Carol, I don't know, but John told me harmful things might happen to you and Mark if something fatal happened to him."

"He told you that?" she asked.

"Yes," David replied. "You and Mark will need protection on your way to DC You are going to Washington, DC, aren't you, Carol?"

She said yes, to which David replied that he and the other agent would drive them. It would be the only way to guarantee their safety. She felt grateful and wanted to call her family to tell them of the plan change. David asked that she wait until they reached Cincinnati. Carol looked at the other agent, Eric Glenn, who hadn't said anything throughout the conversation. She felt uneasy. She didn't trust him, but she didn't know why.

While she and Mark retrieved their luggage from the bus, the two agents rented a car from a lot across the street from the bus station. The four people got into a late-model sedan and rode through Indianapolis. Except for David intermittently reminiscing about his and Johns's initial meeting at the FBI Academy, no one had anything to say. But once they reached Cincinnati, David, who was driving, looked in his rearview mirror and asked Carol, who sat in the backseat with the other agent, "Do you know where the tape is?"

Without looking up from the window, Carol answered calmly, "What tape?"

He stared momentarily but continued, "Didn't John give you a tape to take to DC?"

She was puzzled. "No, David, I don't know about any tape."

David tried to appear undisturbed by the news. He looked over at Mark, who sat in the front passenger seat, and asked half-jokingly, "He didn't give you the tape, did he, buddy?"

The boy said, "Nope, my dad only gave me his lucky duffel bag and my grandfather's baseball glove."

They stopped at a Holiday Inn for the night. Carol was afraid of Eric Glenn. He had worn dark glasses the whole day, said very little, if anything, and put his hand on his gun, hidden beneath his jacket, more than once. Mark slept soundly but she slept uneasily.

The next morning, after breakfast had concluded, she called her mother, who was away at a church function. Her brother Bill answered the phone. She informed him of the day's events regarding the two agents who were accompanying them to DC. Bill wanted to know if she felt safe to continue with them. Carol hesitated in answering but said, "Yes, Bill, and please look for us to arrive this evening."

The four people returned to the car where Carol was once again relegated to the back seat. She recalled the numerous times her husband had told her in his horrible fake Jamaican accent "Bewa de parson who wea de dawk glasses." She remembered laughing at this saying, but laughter was the last thing on her mind right now. She was of the belief that the reason an agent wore dark glasses was to look obscure and inconspicuous—but at night?

As the car proceeded on the Interstate, her long body was becoming increasingly uncomfortable in the back seat. Finally they arrived in Columbus. While keeping an eye on the road, David turned to Carol and asked the same question, "Where's the tape?"

It dawned on her that he was serious. Before she could answer, Eric Glenn pulled the gun from his jacket and put it to her side. "We want the tape," he said gruffly, "or we will hurt you."

Carol stared blankly for a moment then asked, "What

has happened to you, David?" But before he could answer he drove through a red light.

"Man, what are you doing?" Glenn yelled. "We just went through a fuckin' red light!"

"Cool down, man," he replied. "It's a Sunday, and this is a little hick town."

"This little hick *town is Columbus, Ohio," Glenn quickly retorted.*

Mark became startled. Carol said to him in a tight voice, "If anything happens to me, honey, you try to get to DC. You can do it, I know you can."

"Shut up, Carol!" David shouted. His manner was terrifying. When the car slowed for another red light, Carol screamed, "Mark, get out of the car! Now!"

He didn't hesitate. He threw his duffel bag into David's face and the car went out of control and hit a fire hydrant. Eric Glenn's gun went off and Carol slumped into the seat. The boy looked at his mother's limp body and knew she was dead. Then something occurred to him: he would be killed too, if he didn't get out of the car. In what seemed like slow motion, he grabbed his baseball glove and jumped from the car. Before David could open his door to run after him, a police car pulled up beside them. Mark ran away into the maze of homes and trees nearby.

30 years ago -

Carol had been a student at the University of Illinois for five months, and because the school was so large, she was sure she would never get the opportunity to meet a man, much less date one. But one morning, as she was rushing to her first class on her bike, she was barely paying attention when she struck a pedestrian and knocked him down, sending his books in numerous directions. She was overwhelmed with embarrassment and helped the young man get up from the ground.

He shrugged it off as Carol finally calmed down to meet his eyes. She shivered. He was so handsome, and in a letter sweater, he made her stutter. She helped him pick up his books (all eight of them) and wondered why he had so many. "I'm returning these to the library for my frat brothers," he said. "By the way," he continued, "aren't you going to apologize for almost making me a gimp, or at the very least join me for coffee?" He then extended a hand. "My name is John Mason," he said with a twinkle in his eye.

Although she didn't drink coffee, she blurted out the words "Oh yes!" and then caught how stupid she must have sounded and blushed. John remarked that it was refreshing to see a woman blush, and she was really on fire then. Her freckles seemed to take on a hue of their own. "I'm Carol Frazier," she said in between hot flashes.

They wound up cutting classes for the day and spent it talking. She loved his large physique. He loved the way she walked. She thought his hazel eyes were beautiful against his dark brown skin. When he smiled, his dimples seemed to make his face sparkle. "I'm in love," she thought. He thought she had the prettiest legs he'd ever seen. In praising her, he made her blush even more.

Over the next several months, they learned a lot about each other. Although she felt John was somewhat arrogant, Carol also thought he was honest. He was in his senior year at Illinois, and she was a freshman. He was majoring in criminal law and was already accepted at Northwestern University Law School in a northern suburb of Chicago. She wanted to teach. He wanted to become an FBI agent eventually, and she was thrilled. He was twenty-one, and she was eighteen. Their first cup of coffee ended their single lifestyles.

Carol's three brothers seemed stumped when she started dating John, as they never realized their sister had any taste in men. This man they approved of unanimously. John, an only child, felt comfortable with the Fraziers, and her parents liked him as much as she did. Whenever the two were angry with each other, John would still go ahead and play basketball with Carol's brother Carl, also a senior at Illinois. Sometimes, John and Carl would go to the movies or a sports event without her, making her bristle. Carl and John would chuckle. John knew that if he hung around Carl or talked with any member of Carol's family on the phone, she'd hear about it, especially if she was mad at him.

When her father, Larry, died of a heart attack at the end of her sophomore year, John, by that time, heavily involved in law school exams, felt he could not get away to attend the funeral in Washington, DC. Carol was depressed. Although John was now on a different college campus, it was still only a three-hour train ride so they could visit each other most weekends. Although she was only going to be away from school for a week without John, it seemed after two days that she had already been gone for a month. He felt the same way because on the day of the funeral, as they were lowering Larry Frazier's body into the ground, a cab pulled up, and John descended. They embraced without concern for the onlookers, as she knew they were in love.

***

Carol Watson emerged from her past to stare at her current situation—Joel Stover. She was genuinely hoping that Allen Knox did not kill him. Carol felt this young man had been wrestling with his list of demons long enough, and if all it would take to save all of these women was an apology from her husband, Carol knew Howard would give it to him. She looked at Knox before she began her negotiations.

"Mr. Stover…Joel," she began, her voice steady but her heart racing. "Why not release all these women, especially Mrs. Knox and her husband? Then, you can explain why you're so consumed with hatred towards me and my husband that you're willing to sacrifice your young life for this."

Joel's gaze swept over the women, and he could see the fear etched on their faces. They were all terrified, with only a few exceptions. This scenario was different from what he had envisioned.

"No, Mrs. Watson. I can't do that. You see, I need all of these people to know what you and your husband did to me and my family's life after you helped send my father to prison."

Knox had to say something because he had had enough. Otherwise he was going to shoot him.

"Look, Stover, or whatever your name is, my wife needs a doctor. You have a problem with me calling her doctor?"

Joel's eyes were glassy-looking. He started pacing again, this time talking to himself. Xu and Perry glanced at each other, then Knox.

Knox could no longer be quiet. "What the fuck did she and her husband do, for God's sake?!"

Joel pointed his gun at Knox. "Mister, please do not talk again unless you want your baby to be fatherless. Do you understand me?"

Forrestal winced in pain again. Joel became fidgety. Suddenly, the sound of a helicopter could be heard overhead. Joel placed his gun on Carol's back and nudged her over to the window while he peered out. There had to be twenty law enforcement on the lawn. He shook his head. His shoulders went limp.

***

After her phone call with Tim, Callahan quickly got up from her chair and told her girlfriends she had to take care of an emergency and would get back to them another day. They looked at her somewhat confusedly but nodded and began ordering from the menu. She then walked to her car and dialed her phone. Marino and his wife Ellie were lounging in their patio chairs, waiting anxiously for information coming out of Philadelphia. Marino glanced at his phone and saw that it was Callahan calling. He sighed a heavy sigh. He knew she would ask him something he would say no to, so he adjusted his body on the patio chair.

"What can I do for you on a Saturday evening, Callahan?" he asked.

"Director, you've heard about the hostage situation in Philly?"

He sat back in his chair. "Yes, Callahan, I've heard. No, don't ask me. Even Howard would say no."

She was undeterred. "Director, you know I have a background in hostage negotiations. Also…"

"No, Callahan." He shook his head. "I can't allow you to go even if our President signed the papers."

***

Mitchell Butler-Kronen was informed that his regular driver Kevin was on jury duty and that his brother would take his place for a few days. He didn't think anything of this, as he didn't care *who* carted him around as long as *somebody* did. The black Mercedes was waiting for him in front of the elevator doors in the underground parking garage; Butler-Kronen got in. "James, isn't it?"

"Yessir, Mr. Kronen," the driver answered without looking back.

"It's Butler-Kronen, James. I need to stop at our bank before heading in. Wait for me. I should only be twenty minutes."

"Yessir," the voice said again.

"James" then locked the doors, promptly turned around in his seat, sprayed an aerosol into Butler-Kronen's face, and quickly raised the window between the front and back seats. Mitchell-Kronen became unconscious within seconds. Afterward, "James" drove out of the garage, guaranteeing Mitchell Butler-Kronen a different destination.

When Butler-Kronen came to, his wrists and ankles were tied to a chair, and his mouth was duct taped. Two very muscular black men wearing red devil masks stood before him. He thought they were speaking in Arabic, but this was only a guess since Butler-Kronen only knew it wasn't English or any other language he was familiar with. When he was fully conscious, one of the men pulled the duct tape from his mouth.

Butler-Kronen immediately vented his arrogance. "Do you know who I am?" he yelled at the men.

One of the men looked at him through his mask with

piercing eyes. "No, and not care."

Looking around his environment, Butler-Kronen recognized he was in an airport hangar. The room was massive and it was completely empty except for him in the chair and the two men peering over him.

"I am Mitchell Butler-Kronen of the Kronen Group. Where am I? What do you want from me?" he again yelled.

"Mister Butler-Kronen of the Kronen Group," the man said slowly, "shut your trap before we shut it for you. Soon, very soon, you will learn how karma works."

"I have to go to the bathroom," Butler-Kronen urgently yelled. "You will allow me to, right?"

One of the men replaced the duct tape over Butler-Kronen's mouth. Then both men looked at each other and walked away. Butler-Kronen thought perhaps someone, or some group, was going to demand a ransom for his life. He knew his company would pay whatever, but he was worried that even if the company paid, would he escape unhurt, or at all? Butler-Kronen became afraid, his mind racing with terrifying possibilities. In his two-thousand-dollar suit, he then peed on himself.

***

Joel Stover paced the floor with the gun to Carol's back, forcing Carol to walk.

Knox knew that municipal SWAT or FBI SWAT was outside. He had to remain calm, but the helicopter upset his plans. His wife was in pain, and he was about to unleash his anger…but Carol Watson stepped in.

"Joel, if you let me have my phone," she said calmly, "I can call my husband, who can be here in less than two hours.

He can give you what you want if it's an apology."

Joel looked at her, then glanced over at Janet Forrestal, whom he recognized was in legitimate agony. He was about to say something when, outside, the booming voice announced...

"Joel Stover, we know you're in there. The place is surrounded. Why don't you let the women come out, and no casualties will occur?"

Everyone in the room froze.

Joel blew out a breath. "Mrs. Watson, call your husband now."

***

Once Howard was finally able to talk to Carol via the speaker on her phone and was relieved that everyone was unhurt, she relayed what Joel Stover wanted: an apology from him. Howard, torn between his principles and the safety of the innocent, was reluctant to give the young man something he didn't feel was right to give. However, he was in, hoping it would get all the innocent people out of the house, especially Forrestal.

"Let me speak to him, Carol," Howard requested, his voice flushed with worry.

Joel shook his head no. "I want to see Howard Watson in the flesh," he demanded.

"Okay, Stover," he said, "I'll be there in thirty minutes." Howard's voice was firm, showing his unwavering determination to resolve the situation, but the urgency of the matter was not lost on him.

On their way to Knox's house, Howard, Stanton, and Holloway stopped at Penn Medicine, a bustling hospital with its constant stream of ambulances and hurried staff, and picked up Shari Stover, who was still at work.

***

Recognizing after thirty minutes that the two men were not returning, Butler-Kronen chewed on the duct tape to where he could finally utter words.

"HELLLLLOOOO!" he yelled. No answer. He yelled again. Still, no answer. He tried his best to loosen the ropes on his wrists but to no avail. An hour later, two white men, one middle-aged, the other younger, started walking briskly toward him. These were two of his security men.

"Mr. Butler-Kronen!" one yelled.

As they neared him, both men could smell the urine stench emanating from the man they called "sir" in the office.

"How did you find me?" he asked them both.

"Sir," the young man said while untying Butler-Kronen's ropes, "we found Bobby tied up in the garage's maintenance closet. He said two men, whom he believed to be African, but maybe not, grabbed him when he pulled up waiting for you. He said they sprayed something in his face. He also said your car has a tracking device, which is why we are here."

"Was he hurt? What do I care? Fire him because he might be part of this group."

Both men glanced at each other and shook their heads.

"Sir," the middle-aged man remarked, "Bobby has been your driver for seven years. Why would he risk his job by having you kidnapped?"

"I don't care. Get rid of him. He shouldn't have let this happen to me. Were there any demands? Any ransom notes?"

"No sir," the young man answered. We are puzzled by

this scenario."

Butler-Kronen glared at both men. "No one, I mean no one, is to know of this circumstance until we find who did this to me, and why didn't they do anything else except leave me here? One of you grab my extra clothing out of the car's trunk."

He then went throughout the hangar looking for a place to wash the embarrassment off his body.

***

"Joel, it's Mom! Please let me come into the house."

Joel Stover went numb setting up the stage for Carol to step in.

"Joel, before you talk to your mother, please tell me what Howard and I did to make you feel this low. Please."

He held back the tears and talked without hurrying. "When my father went to prison, he wanted no visitors. My grandmother, his mother, suffered a paralyzing stroke. My grandfather, his father, died of a heart attack. My aunt, his sister, was seven months pregnant and miscarried. Her husband divorced her shortly after that. My uncle, my father's baby brother, who saw my father as his mentor and his role model, started taking drugs and eventually OD'd. He was my age when he died…my age. My sister became bulimic, and it took years to pull me from my corner. No one wanted to be friends with my mother— no one, as they thought it was all her fault that my father went to prison. All this happened because my father went to prison, Carol Watson. All because you and your husband sent my father to prison."

Joel then placed the gun on the table. Perry and Xu both

pulled their guns from their backs and pointed them at Stover, who then took a seat on the floor in the corner, and started crying.

Kat Perry, still with her gun pointed at Stover ran to the door and called Howard, who immediately ran into the house followed by Shari Stover who pulled her son off the floor and held him tightly. There wasn't a dry eye in the room. Howard grabbed Carol and then looked at Joel Stover. Xu and Perry replaced their guns behind their backs again.

"Joel, I'm Howard Watson. If it's an apology you need from me and Carol, it's that I'm sorry that your father caused so much pain to you and your family. I hope you get the help that will allow you to move in a positive direction. I mean it, Joel. I cannot talk at length about your father's case but understand that he was responsible for not only shooting Carol, who almost died, but also killing my best friend, her husband, at the time, and his colleague, a decorated war veteran. It was not your fault, nor your sister's fault, and especially not your mother's, that your father went rogue. It was his fault. He caused all this damage, and you should know, from this day forward, that he did all this selfishly. Joel, it was not your fault."

Carol looked at Joel. "It was not your fault."

After being given his Miranda Rights, the Philadelphia Police ushered Joel in the waiting squad car. They told Shari to get a lawyer. Everyone at the shower watched from the windows as the police drove away. Howard then grabbed Carol and held her for a long moment. Forrestal started wincing in pain. Shari Stover, through her tears, ran over to her, announced that the baby was coming, and asked Knox to help her up the stairs to their bedroom.

Twenty minutes later the Knox's welcomed a seven-pound, twelve-ounce baby boy, which, to no one's surprise they named Allen Knox, Jr. Shari Stover was instrumental in the delivery. However, shortly after that, she dashed to make immediate plans for an attorney for Joel. Carol assisted with attorney names. After the birth of baby Knox, the women at the baby shower started breathing freely again, but no one seemed to want to leave. It was strange and it was weird. Although everyone felt sorry for Joel Stover, they were relieved that the scenario had not taken a sinister turn.

***

Mark and his brothers Lawrence and George were all relieved to know that their mom and dad were completely okay. Mark stayed two extra days before heading back to Chicago so that he could visit with his mom.

***

Howard called Tim first. He then called Marino who whistled a sigh of relief while smiling at Ellie.

"I dunno, Al," Howard began, "I suppose young Stover just needed some closure. There is power in apologies and forgiveness."

"Sure, Howard. Too bad he went this route. However, I'll call Phil Davenport in Chicago to apprise him of this incident so that he will allow the Glenn's…er Stover's, to see the file, especially now that Glenn has died."

"What do you think they'll throw at him, Al?"

Marino blew out air. "Howard, you know as much as I do that this is a hostage taker with some mental issues. Stover had only one bullet in the gun, which he might have been prepared to use on himself. However, the judge can impose a prison sentence for any time and up to life in prison. This particular case will probably see young Stover with prison time, but mostly for mental assessment. You and I know that being taken hostage can have lasting effects. It's ironic that all the women interviewed at the shower have said they will be in court on young Stover's day to provide their input that they were not hurt, nor believed they would be hurt."

"Al, you have got to be kidding me."

"Howard, I am not. I've just received a report from Bruce based on the interviews conducted by the hostage negotiators with all the women. The report states that *all the women* have consistently declared, without any external influence, that they believe Joel Stover would never have used his gun. Special Agent Perry and CIA Officer Xu are among the women in this report. Even Forrestal agreed although she declined to be part of the report."

Howard smiled slightly.

"Howard, all this to say this—the women's testimonies are crucial for Stover as they will significantly influence the fairness and equity of the trial for this young man. It's quite a revelation."

One week later –

Dennis Kelvin walked into Frank Leslie's office with news he'd been waiting to report. Howard and Callahan were already seated at Leslie's small conference table, and Leslie was seated at his desk.

"I gotta go back a little," Kelvin said, "so you understand the scope of this situation occurring under our very own eyes."

"Go on," Leslie remarked, looking at Howard.

Kelvin handed the documents to Leslie and Howard and shelled out the information while standing. "The founder of the Carlisle Indian Industrial School in Pennsylvania, one of the earliest federal institutions, loved saying, 'Kill the Indian in him, and save the man.' From 1819 to 1969, the United States took hundreds of thousands of indigenous children away from their parents, sending them to 408 schools across thirty-seven states. By 1926, the federal government had removed more than eighty percent of school-age Indian children from their families. Coincidentally, these same 'socially caring' people established the first animal shelters at the same time. Sorry, I digress."

Howard smiled slightly.

"For many of these children," Kelvin continued, "only time has changed, but not their situation. Many are placed in orphanages not because they don't have any parents but because their parents can't afford to feed them and care for them. When they built the Christian Orphanage for Indigenous Children here in DC in 1950, it was to provide children of color, specifically Native American children, a home. However, based on numerous grievances filed, Christian Orphanage's real intent seems to be forced labor. There have been several disturbing complaints in the past ten years regarding this orphanage, ranging from kids running away but eventually being found to kids never being found, to kids suffering heart attacks.

"Folks at Baltimore General say they have had children admitted from the Christian Orphanage more times than they want to admit. A friend of mine, an ER nurse, says that children as young as ten years old have been admitted for pure exhaustion, almost to the point where they can't stand up without help. By law they have reported to Baltimore Police what they believe is abuse but it seems nothing has destroyed the place. Also, there is a strong belief that children who supposedly ran away and the orphanage have not found them are most likely buried somewhere on the mansion's property. Even with these complaints, it seems nothing has disturbed the Christian Orphanage's ability to stay in business."

Leslie broke in. "How is it funded?'

"In the past decade, the orphanage has received federal grants each year ranging from $25,000 to $75,000 through the Office of Indian Economic Development. This same orphanage has also received hundreds of thousands of dollars from a private foundation called The Kelsy-Wahauser Foundation Group. Get this, The group also funds several other orphanages in Arundel, Chesapeake Beach, and Montgomery, all near tobacco plantations. I was a little shocked to find that the KWG's parent company is the Kronen Group."

Howard looked pleased. So did Leslie.

"Okay," Howard remarked. "Good prelim, Kelvin. We'll let Al know our next move. Callahan, get this report to Al today."

"Yes sir," was all that could escape her lips…that and a smile at Kelvin.

***

Amadi Osman returned to work one week following his "accident." After he dropped the children off at the York Building just like he always did, a male passenger climbed aboard his bus from the back door and sat in the row behind him. Amadi turned around in his driver's seat to speak to him. "I am sorry, sir, but this is a private bus, not for the public."

The man spoke almost in a whispered tone. "Mister Osman, you were given time to think about your injuries. We hope you have come to a conclusion that will satisfy both the Foundation and your family."

With that statement, the man exited the front door of the bus, leaving Amadi Osman stumped for answers.

***

Unaware of Mrs. Osman's urgent message, Sandra Callahan finally received it a week later. The delay was due to a mix-up caused by three secretaries filling in for one on maternity leave. Once Callahan connected with Mrs. Osman, she received shocking news regarding the threatening telephone call. After gathering Kelvin, Callahan hurried to the Osman's residence, a sense of urgency hanging in the air.

Stepping into the Osman's house, Callahan and Kelvin were immediately struck by the sight of young Mr. Osman's injuries from a bus accident a week ago. This time, he didn't ask his parents to leave the room, a move that piqued Callahan's curiosity.

"Agent Callahan," Amadi began. "We are now sure that the Kelsy-Wahauser Foundation is a front for children who are being forced to work. Two companies, Branson Flour and Donahue Tobacco, have these children working in their plants. The regular employees get off work at both companies between two p.m. and two thirty p.m., and the children arrive at three thirty p.m. and work until six thirty or seven thirty p.m. A friend of a friend who works for Branson Flour told me that the regular employees are never asked, or allowed to work overtime. This is because Branson can bring the children in, pay them nothing, and work them like slaves."

Callahan was sold on Mr. Osman's honesty but needed to be convinced of the facts.

"Mr. Osman, how do you know this for sure? I need facts, real…facts. Would this 'friend of a friend' be willing to tell us these same certainties, allowing us to prove the accusations?"

Osman looked at his parents, who offered no rebuttal.

"Agent Callahan," young Osman declared, "we will get you real proof. I promise."

Callahan looked young Osman straight in the eye. "Mr. Osman, I appreciate your offer but cannot condone your putting your life in jeopardy. I will ask my superiors about moving this scenario along. Wait to hear from me. Okay?"

Amadi again looked at his parents, who both nodded in approval. "Okay, Agent Callahan, we'll wait for you."

Both agents left the house without looking back. They knew the family was watching from the window; they were right. As they approached their vehicle, Callahan's attention was caught by the school bus parked in the driveway. It was pristine, with no signs of damage. Osman had claimed his injuries were only a week old, so the bus should have been in repairs, or a substitute should have been in its place. Yet, the license plate was the same, indicating it was the same bus.

***

It was ten p.m. and pouring buckets when Mitchell Butler-Kronen and his two VPs emerged from the banquet and quickly got into the waiting black Mercedes. The driver then locked all the doors, turned around in his seat, and sprayed an aerosol into all three men's faces. He immediately closed the window between the front and back seats and lowered the car door windows in the front seat. The men in the backseat quickly drifted into dreamland.

***

Callahan and Kelvin met with Howard and Frank the following day in Howard's office. Callahan and Kelvin sat on Howard's sofa while Frank and Howard sat at Howard's small conference table. Callahan quickly repeated the phone call made to the Osman's. The caller wanted Amadi to tell the police that the accusations he made about the Kelsy-Wahauser Foundation were erroneous, and he was willing to correct this mistake by signing a document to this effect.

"What did Mrs. Osman do after the phone call?" Howard asked.

Callahan didn't miss a beat. "Mrs. Osman said she called me. The secretary handed me her message, albeit a week late, but Mrs. Osman did call me."

Howard stared at Callahan for a pregnant moment. He felt there was something she wasn't telling him. "What is it, Callahan? What's got your tongue?"

She sat back on the sofa and looked at Kelvin, Frank, and Howard. "Mr. Osman looks like someone or someone's beat him up pretty badly. He says a week ago, his bus was hit by another vehicle, which caused his injuries. I don't believe him. I think his injuries are human made."

Callahan's words hung in the air, heavy with the weight of her accusation.

"Who do you suppose caused these injuries to Mr.

Osman?" Howard asked her.

"I think people contracted through the KW Foundation. The threatening telephone call prefaced young Osman's injuries."

"Why do you believe the Osman's didn't tell you this?" Frank asked.

"Because these Sudanese are a hardy bunch," she said almost matter-of-factly. "I think they are going to take care of the enemy who did this to young Osman themselves. Calling me was just a smokescreen."

Frank's eyes were fixed on Kelvin; his tone was urgent. "I need that bus accident report and the hospital report, Kelvin, today."

After Callahan and Kelvin left Howard's office, Frank went to Howard's window and peered out, lost in thought.

"What are you thinking, Frank?" Howard asked.

Frank turned around to Howard. "I'm thinking we should get one of our people into Branson Flour or Donahue Tobacco."

***

When Butler-Kronen and his two vice presidents awoke, one glanced at his Rolex—it was midnight. They had been knocked out for almost two hours, tied to chairs in a dimly lit, musty room; the only sound heard was water dripping from somewhere. They found it quite unsettling that they could easily untie their ropes. Their tuxedos had been doused with some sour-smelling liquid whose odor mimicked vinegar. The VPs, struggling to comprehend their predicament, were thoroughly confused, but Butler-Kronen, not surprisingly, was livid. He reached for his phone in his jacket pocket. It was still there. He went into his back pants pocket—his wallet was intact, as were the wallets of the other two men. They had no idea where they were. The car was new so it hadn't had a location spotting service installed yet. *Who could have known this?*

The three men ventured outside and found they were in an alley filled with tons of garbage. Several rodents ran past them, making one of the men stiffen so severely he grabbed Butler-Kronen. They ran from the alley into a semi-bustling street. They tried hailing a cab. Three taxis slowed but wouldn't stop. Finally, Butler-Kronen called security at his office, and within ten minutes, a driver, whom Butler-Kronen was familiar with, pulled up, and the three men got in. The driver took them straight to the Kronen Group office, where they took the elevator to the executive floor. Each man remembering he had a shower in his office darted off.

Once they each showered and changed clothes, they met in Butler-Kronen's office. It was one a.m., and after telling their wives the same sappy story of a poker game that could not end, Butler-Kronen sighed and looked at both men.

"We will find out who did this to us, but in the meantime, no one knows of this incident, understand?"

The other two men nodded, understanding the need for utmost secrecy.

"What about the driver?" one man asked.

"We'll handle him—he's on our side."

Donahue Tobacco Company

After some initial reluctance, Marino agreed to Howard's

request and approved Lee for the undercover job. Lee, operating under a cloak of secrecy, assumed the role of a maintenance person at Donahue Tobacco Company. Ahmad Waverly, the techno-wizard, was tasked with creating a device for Kevin to capture the alleged shenanigans at Donahue Tobacco.

The only individual aware of his true identity was a fellow maintenance person, a Chinese friend of the family whose son had worked in his family's laundry. Kevin used him as a reference for the job. This person was warned that surveillance was taking place and that any information he divulged to anyone would land him in Federal prison.

Once inside the massive plant Kevin noticed more than a few Asians working for Donahue, most of them Filipinos. He didn't know there were *any* Asians in the Arundel County area even though it was adjacent to Baltimore. He decided to hang with any older men he saw during his first week of work, especially those who might speak Chinese or Cantonese. Toward the latter part of the week, several employees told him not to ask for overtime.

"They won't give it," an older Black man said, implying that the company was not generous with overtime.

"How come?" Kevin asked.

The man shrugged his shoulders and walked away. Kevin, determined to discover more, believed the man's eyes signaled that he was trustworthy. He thought maybe the older man knew something. He would check with him another day.

＊＊＊

After working at Donahue for two days, Kevin met with Howard and Tim in Howard's office to discuss any action or eye-opening scenarios, but thus far, he had seen none. His uniform, bearing the Donahue Tobacco logo, was a reminder of the environment he was observing. He removed this shirt then put on a T-shirt in Howard's office bathroom.

"Tell us what you know, Kevin," Tim asked.

"The mostly male employees punch in at six a.m.," he began. "The assembly line jobs are given two fifteen-minute breaks and a thirty-minute lunch. They punch out like robots at two p.m."

"What time do you work?" Howard asked him, trying not to smile.

He ignored Tim's and his smiles and delivered their answer with ease.

"There are two divisions of maintenance. One begins at six thirty, and I start at seven thirty a.m. The earlier maintenance punches out at one thirty p.m., and my division punches out at two thirty p.m. Any more questions because I am beat?"

"Yeah, we get it," Tim added. "These types of jobs help us stay humble. Anything else, because Ahmad is on his way here to brag about his latest invention for you."

"Well, the plant is not just large, it's massive, and probably houses hundreds of employees. Since I'm in maintenance, I pretty much have the privilege of exploring every part of this colossal structure except the shipping department. However, the shipping department caught my attention. It's a wing in the warehouse where the machines place the cigarettes in boxes for shipping. I can't help but wonder about the people who work there and the conditions they work in. When do these people work, I asked myself."

"You mean you haven't seen anyone in the shipping department in two days?" Howard asked.

"First of all," Kevin remarked, "I'm not allowed in that department to clean—only seniority are allowed. Secondly, I snuck over there late this afternoon, and still no people, although the lights are on, and so are all the machines."

A knock was heard at the door.

"This should be Ahmad," Tim said.

***

The Osman family gathered at the daughter's house again to discuss their plan to stop Mitchell Butler-Kronen and his bullies from continuing their threats to Amadi. The family felt no alternative but to begin a severe turn of events.

***

Mitchell Butler-Kronen glared at his four security men.

"Who the hell is doing this to us, to me?" he screamed.

The oldest of the men answered. "Sir, we are working with cameras, employees, and any other avenues of exposure to flush out the person or group perpetrating these acts, sir."

"Well, until we catch this person, or persons, only you four can drive me. Is that understood?"

All four men agreed in unison.

***

Sandra Callahan met with Howard and Frank Leslie in Howard's office. Dennis Kelvin had provided additional information on the Kelsy-Wahauser Foundation and the Kronen Group and she wanted them to learn of the latest news.

"Several strange happenings occurred in the past week regarding Mr. Mitchell Butler-Kronen. I received these two photos—one of Butler-Kronen roped and tied to a chair in what looks like an airport hangar…" She handed the photo to Howard. "And this second one of Butler-Kronen and two other men, yet to be identified, roped and tied to chairs in what looks like an empty garage or storage."

She handed the second photo to Howard, who sat back in his chair and tried not to smile. He gave both photos to Leslie.

"I take it Mr. Butler-Kronen is okay? I mean, we haven't heard anything to the effect that he was kidnapped, or he's into bondage-type games. Where did you get these, Callahan?"

"They were delivered to me specifically, Howard, as you can see on the envelope by the US Postal Service, with no sender's return address. Also, checking on Butler-Kronen— Kelvin said he saw him enter his office this morning so he's obviously alive."

"Who do you think sent these?"

"If I were a bettin' gal, I'd say someone from the Osman family."

"What is going on?" Frank chimed in.

"Frank, someone or someone's beat up our dear little Osman. Probably a contract through the Kelsy-Wahauser Foundation or from the Kronen Group. Betting again, I will put my money on Butler-Kronen himself."

"*Mitchell Butler-Kronen*? You've got to be kidding."

"Not kidding, Frank."

Frank shook his head downward.

"I think Fleischman's wife plays golf with Mrs. BK."

"Oh, man," Howard quipped. "This doesn't look good."

Callahan shook her head. "Can't help how it looks, Howard."

"So you think *Mitchell Butler-Kronen* knows underage children work at one or several of his client's plants, and the clients can't seem to produce their significant profits without making these children enslaved people? Am I on the right track, at least?"

"Right train, too."

"Well, Al has to know about this latest situation," Frank added. "Especially since we now know that Mr. Osman's injuries were not due to any bus accident. The Mercy Medical Center report showed him last week as an ER admittance at midnight with a busted lip, chipped tooth, black eye, and a broken wrist. He refused an overnight stay."

"Well, we're hoping Kevin unearths something significant at the Donahue Tobacco Company. That's one of Kronen Group's clients right, Callahan?"

"Yes Howard, it is."

Alberto Marino's conference room

As always, Marino and the rest of the team were filled with confidence regarding Ahmad's latest engineering marvel. As he stood in front of the group, Ahmad handed Marino a small black apparatus the size of Marino's thumb. Marino inspected what looked like a piece of woven rope and passed it on to the others in the room.

"I've embedded this tiny black lithium device into the

Donahue Tobacco logo on Kevin's three work shirts." Ahmad said. "The apparatus can capture audio with near-perfect clarity if Mila remains dry. I call her Mila, short for "minuscule interlocking apparatus."

Everyone smiled.

"The challenge? Each recorder has a lifespan of ten hours, so Kevin has to seek me out daily before time runs out. He must also hand-wash these shirts because the logo can't get wet. The plan…"

He was interrupted by Kevin raising his hand. Ahmad nodded, giving him the floor.

"I recognize that my Chinese background includes a family-owned laundry, but I have never ventured into the realm of handwashing anything in my entire life, and now you assign me *this* task?"

The room erupted in laughter.

"Sorry, Kevin," Ahmad said insincerely. He then reached into a backpack in the empty chair next to him and took out a USB cord and something similar looking to a stovetop burner. "Here's the plan Kevin. You bring me a shirt each late afternoon. In return, I'll place the shirt pocket logo on this metal plate, which is connected to this USB source. The 'plate' will then produce sound through my computer, effectively recharging the lithium battery for its subsequent use."

"Waverly, this is pretty good," Marino voiced, "but where is the challenge in only capturing audio and no video?"

"Director, since the plant is massive, connectivity problems or bandwidth limitations will probably affect video data. Unfortunately, we must depend on Agent Lee's memory as to who is talking."

Marino shook his head, prompting Howard to add to the

sketchy picture.

"Al, you know as well as I do that inadequate lighting conditions can also impact video quality."

Marino looked at both men.

"I'm sure it will work, but I must run it past John. Waverly, can you set up this device—sorry, apparatus—tomorrow morning so John can approve this plan?"

Ahmad looked at Tim, then Howard, who nodded. "Sure, Al, sure."

"Another thing," Marino added, "once John learns that our person of interest is Mitchell Butler-Kronen, he will probably hit the ceiling. I need as much proof as you can get me."

Everyone agreed.

Marino wasn't done. "Callahan, shadow the young Osman fellow for a couple of days. See where he goes and what he does when he drops off the kids at various places."

"Yes, Al," she said, looking at Frank, who nodded to Dennis Kelvin.

"Hamilton, shadow Mitchell Butler-Kronen."

"Sure, Al," he responded.

"Lee, get me some proof!"

Kevin nodded vigorously.

"Hamilton and Lee, keep in touch with Yamamoto. Tim, stay in touch with Howard."

Tim nodded. Howard, and probably Frank got a kick out of Marino assigning jobs, which he only did when bored. However, Marino's authority was unquestioned.

"Howard, you and Frank meet me in my office. Everyone else, dismissed."

***

After the crew had gone, Marino walked to his big picture window and stared out at the setting sun. Frank and Howard looked at each other and then back at Marino.

"What's up, Al?" Howard remarked.

"Take a seat. Joel Stover's trial is in six weeks. Surprisingly, Howard, your wife has decided to be a witness for the defense…"

"Not really a surprise."

"I'm not finished. CIA Officer Xu and Philadelphia Agent Katherine Perry are among the twenty-two women at the shower, who, if called, will speak on Stover's behalf. The problem is Knox."

"Allen Knox?" Howard asked.

"Same fellow. He's being called a witness for the prosecution."

"What?"

"Knox believes Stover placed a heavy burden on Forrestal, and whether Stover intended to use his gun or not, no matter that there was only one bullet, Knox believes his wife's life and the life of his unborn baby at the time was in peril."

"Whoa."

"I recognize Knox is your friend, Howard, but you cannot talk to him about this case, especially since your wife is working the other side of the fence."

Marino's words hung in the air.

Frank was impatient with the banter. "I'm in a fog here guys, bring me up to date, please."

"Howard, you want to tell this or you want my unbiased narrative?"

Howard shook his head. "You tell it, Al."

Marino took a seat at his desk, opened a drawer and took out a cigar, which he quickly ran across his top lip. Howard and Frank then moved from his conference table to the sofa, knowing they were in for a probably precise, but long story.

"Fifteen years ago, Howard's wife, then Carol Mason, was married to a Chicago field office agent named John Mason. Also out of the Chicago office were two of Mason's colleagues, David Snell and Eric Glenn. The two latter men were found *partly* responsible for the deaths of John Mason and a decorated retired helicopter crew chief in the US Army named Carl Sunderland."

"I was in Quantico when I heard this story, Al. But go on."

"Glenn and Snell were *completely* responsible for the kidnapping of Carol Mason and her then ten-year-old son Mark in order to retrieve a tape both men thought Mason had given his wife or son. This tape, later recovered, detailed all that I'm about to tell you."

He ran the cigar across his upper lip again. "Carol and Mark were unaware that Mason had placed this hugely recriminating tape in Mark's baseball glove, a glove his grandfather had given him years prior to his passing. Mason mentioned to his wife that if anything happened to him they would have to urgently seek out his colleague, the famous Howard Watson, for their safety. So they decided to move to DC, which is where Carol is from originally. Under the pretense of helping Carol and Mark get to DC from Chicago safely and unhurt, Snell and Glenn offered to drive them. When Carol recognized that neither she nor Mark knew what the agents were referring to in reference to any tape, Carol knew their lives were in danger. Glenn was holding a gun on

Carol at the time, and the car they were riding in went through a red light in Ohio and hit a major pothole making the gun go off and shooting Carol in the abdomen.

"Mark, thinking his mother was dead, was able to escape from the car and run into a flood of neighborhoods. He then tried getting to DC by hitching rides or walking, trusting no one."

"Mark walked, if I remember," Frank broke in.

Howard nodded.

"Yes." Marino smiled. "Which is why he is my godson."

Howard smiled and shook his head.

"Anyway," Al continued, "Ohio State Police in Columbus stopped the car because it went through a red light, saw Carol's slumped body, and arrested Snell and Glenn. Through candid testimony, both scamps had informed the US Attorney's office, in exchange for lighter sentences, that two CIA operatives hired them and two US Senators who went by the names "Leopold and Loeb" hired the CIA officers. All to retrieve a tape. It was a big mess."

He paused. "Frank, you can find all this info listed as FOI."

"Nah, Al, I like your rendering."

Both Howard and Marino smiled.

"Of course," Marino continued, "the two CIA operatives were thrown under a bus before they walked into a courtroom. They wouldn't name names, but the probability of senators from Arizona, Colorado, Nebraska, and Texas is high since those are big defense contract states. Coincidentally, two of these probable senators did not seek reelection, claiming age was getting in the way."

Howard added his part. "Snell said that these contract companies wanted to see the US a power again after 9/11, and to them that meant a greater buildup of defense hardware. According to Snell, the administration at that time was weakening American military might worldwide. It did not favor stepping up arms contracts, which meant billions of possible dollars to these companies.

"This was an administration run by a squeaky-clean president, wife, and two sons. So, to get the president's attention, the CIA leaked information about the president's wife being a lesbian to the media. The story said the president's wife was caught several times in an uncompromising position with a female senior military officer based at the White House. This 'person of interest' was no longer based at the White House when the story aired and the press was told that the president paid to have the person of interest deployed elsewhere.

"The president's ratings plummeted. The story was false, but the damage had been done and the president was not reelected."

Marino took it from there. "Brad Nelson in the U.S. Attorney's Office said the CIA employed secret efforts to influence numerous events abroad, but they just couldn't budge the president. Although I hate to admit this because the FBI has been wrong in certain covert operations, but even Watergate, which revealed widespread wrong-doing by the FBI, was partly engineered by former CIA employees."

Marino put the cigar back in its humidor and closed the drawer. "Snell was killed in prison within three months of his incarceration, and Glenn died two weeks ago in prison, a week before he would be released. Both men left scorched earth with their involvement. This scorched earth is what Glenn's son Joel Stover has been walking on."

***

Kevin Lee reported to his job at Donahue Tobacco promptly at seven thirty a.m. His Chinese colleague was in front of him at the clock, for which they punched in. They would meet later at lunch. The older Black man who told Kevin not to ask for overtime was behind him in the line.

"So you're still here, eh?" the man asked.

"Looks that way," Kevin answered. He then punched the clock and started walking toward the Maintenance Department.

The man decided he wanted to impart some advice. "The name's Chester Davis," he said, pointing to his ID.

Kevin shook the extended man's hand. "Nice to meet you, Chester. I'm Kevin Lee."

"Same, Kevin. Now, I'm only saying this so you don't get written up or let go, but 'cause you're new here, don't hang with people who smile in your face. Listen to them talk first. You know the song 'Backstabbers,' right?"

"No, I don't believe I know that song—who's it by?"

The older man shook his head and walked away. Kevin watched him with a seemingly look of disappointment on his face. *All because I don't know that song?*

Kevin then walked past the shipping department and was surprised to see numerous people boxing cigarettes and others wheeling the boxes to the trucks. His gaze lingered a moment too long as an older male employee, sensing his curiosity, looked at his identification tag hanging around his neck.

"I recognize from your ID that you're new here, so let me be clear. Your tag states the departments you're responsible for—this isn't one of them. You're not supposed to be in this area. Get me?" he said, his authority detectable, encouraging Kevin to get the message.

"Sorry," Kevin said, his insincerity practically dripping from his lips. "I'm on my way."

Kevin walked away without looking back. He also etched the supervisor's name—Chris Plummer—in his memory file.

***

When Kevin met with Ahmad three days without anything to report, Dennis Kelvin came through with a background on Christopher Plummer, which he forwarded to Kevin.

Kevin then met with Howard in Tim's office. He read from the document. "Christopher Plummer was born in and grew up in Belleview, Illinois, across the Mississippi from St. Louis, Missouri. He should be about forty now, but when he was twenty-six, he did six years in the Illinois Department of Corrections for Armed Robbery."

"What did he rob?" Tim asked.

"A gas station and a liquor store."

"Did he use a gun?"

"Yes."

"How long has he been with Donahue?" Howard asked.

"A little over six years," Kevin answered.

"So this could be a guy who's turned himself around or a guy who knows all about the underage children working in the plant," Tim added.

Both men nodded in agreement.

"So, Kevin, it's crucial that you find out which one is he, our friend or our foe?"

Philadelphia, PA

Once Janet strolled off to the bedroom with the baby in tow, Howard knew Knox was going to grill him regarding the upcoming Stover case. They walked into the kitchen.

"I don't understand why we can't discuss this, Howard," Knox said, pointing to a barstool.

"It's not that simple, Knox. You're a witness for the prosecution, Carol for the defense, and I'm caught in the middle as the arresting officer."

The complexity of the situation was hanging in the air and the tension in the room was thick, each word adding to the weight of the situation.

"Howard, do you seriously think I should just let this go?" Knox's voice trembled with the weight of his dilemma.

"Can't answer that, Knox. Grab me a bottle of water out of your fridge."

Knox went to his refrigerator, got two bottles of water, and handed one to Howard. He heard a scream, which was all an infant could communicate. "Yeah, he takes after Janet," Knox noted.

Both men laughed.

"Look, Knox, I recognize that *you feel* you were not protecting your wife, your mother, Janet's mother, and the other women in that room. But remember, even Perry and Xu never felt the need to brandish their weapons. *All* the women, including Kelly Yamamoto, have agreed and will not testify against Stover. Simple. Done."

"Howard, that's not enough to stop me," Knox declared, his voice unwavering.

Howard took a swig from his water bottle, placed it on the counter, and headed for the front door. "Unless you want to talk about anything else, we're done here, Knox. Kiss Janet and the baby for me. I'm flying back to DC."

With that, he turned and left, his departure marking the end of their conversation.

***

Howard learned several days later from Carol that the Pennsylvania Department of Corrections was transferring Joel Stover to a mental health facility. She explained by addressing his underlying mental health issues first, he would be able to stand competently at trial, making it easier for any judge to see that with treatment, there was a real potential for Joel to reintegrate into society if he were to be released. Carol and others thought this was a reason for optimism about his future.

Knox was furious.

Howard remained composed, holding his breath as he listened to Knox rant on his speakerphone at his desk. His calm demeanor starkly contrasted Knox's escalating emotions, which Howard found troubling as Knox was rarely angry about anything.

"Howard, you have got to be kidding me! They're going to let this crazy guy go free when he could have killed, maimed, or caused someone a stroke pointing his gun?"

Knox's voice was filled with frustration, his words echoing the intensity of the situation.

"No, Knox, I'm not kidding. This young man was struggling with his demons. He chose to unload them on Carol and me, but he picked the worst possible moment, at the baby shower. If Forrestal hadn't been pregnant, or if she hadn't been at the shower at all, would you still be so consumed by anger for the other women in that room?"

Howard's voice was calm, but there was an edge to it.

"But Howard, she *was* at the shower."

***

Since Gina Stover was still attending college, she and her mother took turns visiting Joel. The drive was only forty minutes, but it seemed to Shari, especially, that it took longer. She was able to talk to Joel through a thick glass window. He looked strangely content. Shari, with her medical background, recognized the signs of someone in suicidal mode. But as Joel's mother, her concern for his well-being was paramount. She was determined to nurture him until the darkness disappeared. She didn't care how long it took; she would see it through. Her true wish at this time was to dig up her former husband and bury him again.

***

Callahan followed Amadi Osman in her car all day without his knowledge. Finally, at the end of his day, he dropped off six children at the York Building and drove away. Callahan waited fifteen minutes, took off her blazer, took her braid out, ratted her hair, put on red lipstick and sunglasses, and walked into the York Building. She looked around for five minutes and noted no one was around. She yelled for somebody…anybody…but no one answered. Finally, a very young Native American girl walked into the reception area. Callahan asked if she knew where everyone was, but the girl shook her head and hurried to the bathroom, leaving Callahan alone in the vast space. As she cautiously ventured toward some doors down a hall, a middle-aged man appeared, seemingly out of nowhere, catching her off guard.

"Ma'am, can I help you? Are you looking for someone?" he asked.

Callahan braced herself. "Is this the place with an afterschool program? I have a full-time job and need a place for my two kids to go before I can pick them up from work. What ages do you take? What do you charge, and will you accept two new kids?"

The man was bombarded with so many questions at once that he was visibly uncomfortable, his unease noticeable. "Ma'am, you need to talk to the director 'cause he makes all the rules."

"Well, where is the director, and where is everyone? I've been calling and yelling, and nobody's around. Where're the kids?"

The man then called someone on his cell phone, speaking in hushed tones and casting glances at Callahan. A man emerged on the scene within minutes.

"I'm sorry, Miss…"

"Ms. Damon," Callahan asserted.

The man extended his hand. "Ms. Damon, Vernon Channing. Sorry to keep you waiting. You were asking where the children are. They are either on the playground or in the rooms doing homework. Can I show you around?"

Callahan was surprised at this move. How did he know she was asking about the children? Perhaps it was a code between the two men. Without hesitation, she agreed to the tour.

***

Donahue Tobacco Company, a long-standing presence in Arundel County with a sixty-year legacy, underwent a significant and entirely unexpected change in leadership five years ago. Alger Donahue appointed his then thirty-five-year-old grandson Conrad Donahue, a trust fund baby with no business experience, as the new CEO. This surprising turn of events was a result of Alger's son's refusal to take on the role, leading to the unexpected appointment of Conrad.

Unlike his father, Conrad was easily swayed into various negative situations. He graduated from high school with top scores on his SATs and ACTs, a feat he achieved by paying a "friend" to sit for him. His college years were a breeze, thanks to his grandfather's influence. His mother, hailing from an equally affluent family, played a significant role in shaping his character and made sure all his needs were met.

So the idea of children working for Donahue, whom Conrad was told no one really cared about, was easily achieved because he believed police could be bought off, and they were. His grandfather was incredibly proud of the profits which started soaring during young Donahue's reign.

***

Christopher Plummer, Shipping Department Supervisor, was ushered into Conrad Donahue's office and sat on his sofa. Donahue glanced at his watch and then offered Plummer a cigarette, which he took two and placed one behind his ear.

"Well, what do you want, Plummer, since you said it was necessary to see me today?"

Plummer glanced around the office. "I believe there's a mole in the plant."

"What do you mean, mole?"

"Someone's been leaking information about the kids to the cops again. I think it's someone from the inside."

Donahue sat up straight in his chair.

Plummer continued. "We have several new people working in shipping. This is the first time I have heard of them. Who are they? Where did they come from?"

"Don't worry. They've been thoroughly screened, and their activities are being closely monitored."

"I also saw a Chinese-looking guy who just started in maintenance snooping around in shipping. He was acting like he was looking for something specific. He might have been lost, but where did he come from? We can't afford someone to compromise the operation."

"Plummer, HR is beneath me asking about employees. I'm only interested in those who work in shipping. Check around on the two new people in shipping, then get back to me. Also, don't come to my office again unless you have an appointment. Is that clear?"

Plummer got up from the couch, stubbed out his cigarette in Donahue's marble ashtray on his desk, and left the office without so much as a goodbye.

***

The package arrived while Mitchell Butler-Kronen's Executive Assistant was away from her desk. It came without fanfare, like all the other packages she received throughout the day. The EA opened it like she did all the packages. The sudden blast of red powder from the package over her face, hair, and clothing caused a wave of panic, making her and the two secretaries scream in horror.

Mitchell Butler-Kronen stepped outside his office suite when he heard the screams.

"What happened?" he yelled.

The EA could only shake her head. To their credit, two security guards were on the scene in minutes.

"Did you see who delivered this package?" one guard asked the EA.

She shook her head and looked over at the secretaries, who also shook their heads.

"I just returned from my break, and the package was here. The rest of these packages and mail were already on my desk."

"Anything else in the package?" Butler-Kronen asked.

The security guard picked it up, and inside was a card. He read, "Paprika looks like dried blood, doesn't it?"

"What?" Butler-Kronen yelled.

"That's what the card says, sir," the guard said.

"What does it say on the package?"

The guard read what was on the address. "Mitchell Butler-Kronen, CEO, The Kronen Group."

"No return address?"

"No, sir."

The two VPs, victims of a recent scenario involving them and Butler-Kronen, looked at each other.

"Mitch, let's step into your office." one said adamantly.

Butler-Kronen looked at his EA. "I'm sorry, Shirley, that this tomfoolery happened to you. Go clean yourself up and take the rest of the day off."

"Yes, sir," she said as she grabbed her purse from her drawer and locked her desk. The two secretaries exchanged worried glances, unsure of what to do next.

He looked at the security guards. "Get maintenance up

here to clean up this mess."

"Mitch," one VP explained, "someone is trying to break you down."

"I know, but who do you suppose is trying to do this to me?"

"What about that bus driver?"

"Are you kidding me?" Butler-Kronen said almost arrogantly. "He's just a cog in a wheel. Speaking of, has he signed the document?

"No, not yet, but he just returned to his job. Should we keep on him?"

"Your guys roughed him up a bit too much. Don't let them go overboard this time. Just let him know this is the last warning."

"Yes, Mitch. By the way, a Christopher Plummer is here to see you."

"Who? What does he want? Let him wait."

The two VPs left his office and Butler-Kronen sat at his desk and turned around in his chair to face the lunchtime crowd in the city of Washington, DC. He then lit up a cigarette.

The EVP, who hadn't been involved in the Butler Kronen shenanigans, was busy making a call on his cell phone in his office, detaching himself from the chaos.

"Yes," he confirmed to the caller on the other end of the line, "I agree, this is crucial. Yes, sir, I will keep you updated on the outcome."

He then placed his cell phone on his desk, strode to his window, and gazed out at the midafternoon sun, his mind buzzing with anticipation for what was to come.

***

Brett Hamilton shadowed Butler-Kronen's car for an entire day, his presence unnoticed. Ahmad's skill was evident as he placed a MILA device on Brett's front license plate and Butler-Kronen's vehicle's back license plate. This device allowed Brett to eavesdrop on conversations in the back seat as long as he stayed within three cars' distance. However, the device's battery life was a concern, with Brett nearing the end of his seven-hour surveillance and nothing raising a flag. He would try again the next day.

***

Callahan went straight to Howard's office after she toured the York Building and its grounds. When she arrived, Howard, Frank, and Tim Yamamoto were all in Howard's office. They were somewhat amused at her altered appearance but impressed at her initiative. Although Howard knew Marino would not be pleased with this stunt, he thought her findings could lead to significant benefits, so he decided only to mention it to Marino if he had to. He nodded to Callahan to share her information.

"When I first walked in," she said, "no one, I mean no one, was in the lobby or reception area, which is quite large. I probably yelled for assistance two to three times before someone came to my aide."

"Was there any laughter or children's noises of any kind?" Frank asked her.

"No, as a matter of fact, it was almost eerie quiet. After about ten minutes, I was going to open some doors I saw down a hall when someone finally joined me."

"Was it a security person?" Howard asked.

"I really can't tell you, Howard, but he did make a call to someone, and that someone came on the scene within minutes."

"What about the someone?"

"Vernon Channing, white, blond, late fifties, maybe…had on a white shirt with the 'Kelsy-Wahauser Foundation' logo on the left pocket."

"What happened next?"

"He showed me around the Foundation, the five classrooms, a small library with several computers, and the grounds with outdoor playground equipment. Maybe twenty-five to thirty children were all nestled in their various spots, including the children Amadi Osman dropped off."

Howard stared at Frank and Tim. All three men shook their heads in a perplexed and confusing way as they tried to make sense of Callahan's reporting.

"Something's not right," Tim remarked.

"I agree," Frank added, nodding in affirmation.

"I felt the same," Callahan added, "but Channing couldn't possibly know I was anything but a parent looking for a place for my kids. After the tour, he told me they didn't have any openings, but certainly I should check back in two to three months."

Tim shook his head.

"Callahan, don't you get it? You're a white woman, probably with white kids. This group is only interested in children of color…children with no obvious means of protection. We have to go after this bunch, Howard."

"I have to talk with Al first, who has to get approval from Fleischman. Let's see how far John wants any of us involved. Al will have to mention Kevin's undercover work is still ongoing at Donahue."

Alberto Marino's office

It did not go over well with John Fleischman.

"This is all based on circumstantial evidence," he began. "This was not information obtained based on first-hand experience by this bus driver. He was only guessing by what he believed he witnessed illegally occurring."

Marino listened to his protest as much as he could.

"John," Marino insisted, his voice suggesting frustration, "Mr. Osman affirmed the words used to him were 'recant your statements about the foundation for your safety and that of your family' were pretty clear. If you recall, he received a rather severe beating after telling the police what he believed to be true about the Foundation."

Fleischman dug in to the possibility that Marino and his colleagues could actually be wrong about this probe.

"We don't know if the Foundation had anything to do with his injuries, only that Mr. Osman said they did. It's Mr. Osman's word against a slew of well-heeled men of high status in this city and that of Arundel County. Al, you know as well as I do that we need proof before I contact the DOJ.

"You bring me proof, and I'll move this scenario along."

***

Marino gathered his troops. They met in his conference room—Howard, Frank, Tim, Ahmad, Callahan, Brett, Kevin, and Dennis Kelvin. No one looked excited.

"I've spoken with John," he began, "and it seems that we need actual proof of Mr. Osman's accusations that the Kelsy-Wahauser Foundation is involved in placing underage children in illegal, unsafe, and hazardous positions at one, possibly two locations while ruining their young lives."

Howard and Frank glanced at each other, wondering where Marino was going with his rant. Marino then got up from his chair and walked to his window. He continued talking while looking outside. "Just because I'm in this job does not mean I am looking to punish others. However, it does mean I care about people's safety from criminal activities. I especially care about children's safety."

He turned around and looked at both Howard and Frank. "I…we…need as much proof as we can get regarding the scum treating these children like they are nothing. I believe Mr. Osman's statements. However, we want to ensure that we are not in any way embarrassed about the outcome of this probe if it sends a CEO, Chief of Police, or the Mayor of Baltimore to prison based on our absolute proof of labor trafficking. Do you two read me?"

Both men nodded as if to say, yeah, we read you.

With this last statement, the men were dismissed.

***

Frank and Tim met later in Howard's office. Howard looked at the two men sitting and facing him at his desk.

"Let's see where we are with this case. We have *no* concrete evidence to back up Mr. Osman's allegations. Number two, we all believe Osman. Number three, Callahan is sure something besides mismanagement is happening at that Foundation, but what? Number four, Kevin hasn't produced any evidence of wrongdoing at Donahue Tobacco. So, what's next?"

"Howard," Frank asked, "what's your guy's name at Baltimore Field Office, the Black supervisor?"

"Terrence Millhouse?"

"Yes, he's the one. We need him and the Baltimore office right now."

Tim looked confused, but Howard smiled and shook his head in affirmation. "Frank, you're a credit to your gender."

***

Try as he might, Kevin could not elicit any conversations at lunchtime about the reasons for no overtime. Most employees just shrugged their heads at the mention. Others got up from the conversation and walked away—except Chester Davis. He motioned to Kevin to walk with him outside while he lit a cigarette.

"The reason you can't get overtime is that DT…Donahue Tobacco, has children working for them once we leave the property."

"What are you talking about, Chester? What children? Whose children?"

"I don't know whose children. All I know is that they are children. My friend had worked here for almost six years and saw the children bussed. She told HR, and suddenly, she was fired because we have an "employee at will" contract we signed before we were employed. Didn't you sign one?"

"Yes, I did. So she told HR? How do you know this?"

"She told some of us she was going to HR to tell them about it. We didn't see her after that."

"Aren't you afraid of telling me this? You could be

fired?"

"Man, I'm sixty-seven. Social Security is calling my name. Also, my wife got a nice pension from the post office. I just don't want to see you let go because you don't know the rules."

"I appreciate it, Chester. Was the woman fired Chinese?"

Chester laughed. "Naw, man, Gwen ain't in no way Chinese."

This information was music to Kevin's, and later, Ahmad's ears.

FBI Baltimore Field Office, Baltimore, MD

Howard and Frank met Terrence Millhouse in his office. After introductions died down, Howard carefully described the possible labor trafficking situation. Millhouse bobbed his head several times during Howard's description of the situation.

"Howard, we've known about Donahue Tobacco, Branson Flour, and Christian Orphanage for several years now. We just can't seem to get anyone to talk. Nobody wants to lose their job, so nobody talks. I was thinking, since you used Agent Callahan to enter the Foundation, and Agent Lee is at Donahue, what if we use our agent here, David Martinez? He could do at Branson what Lee is doing at Donahue. This way, we will have three-way proof of activities. What say you, Howard?"

Howard and Frank were pleased with the idea. They knew that if they could just get this idea past Marino and Gerry Kramer, Millhouse's boss, for approval, it could significantly impact the labor trafficking situation.

***

Janet Forrestal opened the door to a wonderful surprise—Carol Watson. As soon as Carol washed her hands and placed the mask over her mouth, she gurgled along with the four-week-old bundle of joy in her arms.

"I'm sorry to be visiting while Allen is on assignment, but Janet, it's you I'm here to visit."

Carol's unexpected words hung in the air, a sudden twist in the otherwise ordinary day. Forrestal looked at Carol and fully understood the reason for the visit. She knew that if anyone was going to change Knox's mind about not prosecuting Joel Stover, it would be the two of them.

Gibson Island, MD

Gibson Island was a gated community, limiting access to the island and its facilities to residents or those with a reason for visiting. Many residents of the island were seasonal who resided primarily in Washington, DC, or Baltimore. The home prices on the island started at $1 million, with the median sale price being $2.5 million. This made Gibson Island the most expensive zip code in Maryland. It's part of Anne Arundel County in Maryland and home to James Butler-Kronen, Jr., who was in his den when his wife knocked on the door and told him with a smile that he had a visitor.

He wheeled his chair around from his desk to face the

visitor. It was Gavin Henderson, his former EVP from the Kronen Group. James, Jr. greeted him with a hint of anticipation.

"Gavin, good to see you in the flesh."

The man hurried to shake Butler-Kronen's hand. He responded in a respectful tone. "I feel the same, Jim."

"Do you men need anything?" Butler-Kronen's wife asked.

"No, honey. We'll be fine. Besides, if Gavin needs anything to drink, I have my trusty cabinet here to help us out."

With that comment, Mrs. Butler-Kronen closed the door and left the room.

***

Brett decided on a change of course—to follow Butler-Kronen in the evening. It was a good decision as he watched his security detail change drivers and three men, in addition to Butler-Kronen, get into the black Mercedes waiting for them in front of the Kronen Group building. A few miles away, the driver dropped off the group at an upscale restaurant, where they stayed for two hours. The black Mercedes remained parked a few yards down the street. Before the men came out of the restaurant, two very muscular Black men pulled the driver, who was smoking a cigarette, out of the Mercedes, knocked him out and placed him in the trunk of another car. The Mercedes then pulled up in front of the restaurant, and Butler-Kronen and his cronies got in. Brett then called Tim and told him he was following the car. Brett then noticed the vehicle turn into an alley. Tim told him that he would call backup but Brett had already hung up. Brett then parked his car yards from the alley, made sure his Glock was secured around his ankle, and wandered into the alley, fully aware of the potential danger that might lie ahead. He texted Tim on his cellphone to inform him of his whereabouts and the looming threat.

The two very dark-skin muscular men now wore red devil masks. They carried all four seemingly unconscious passengers into an empty garage, which looked as if it hadn't been in use for decades. A light went on, and Brett could see through a filthy window that based on his apparel, one of the unconscious men was a priest. They were then tied up to chairs and doused with some liquid on their pants legs. The four men started to come to, and the two muscular men held what looked like cigarette lighters in front of them. Brett could not read their lips, wishing Callahan had been with him, but he could tell that the two muscular men were getting ready to set the captives on fire.

"If you do not stop tormenting children right now," one of the men said adamantly, "we will flood you with karma. Do you understand me?"

Butler-Kronen did not hear a word the man said. "Who are you, and do you know who we are?"

Muscular man number one flicked his cigarette lighter on the pants leg of the priest. The man screamed horrifyingly. The snapping sound of the fire made the other men cry. The air quickly filled with the scent of burning skin and clothing.

Brett didn't know what to do. He started pacing wildly.

Muscular man number two quickly produced a fire extinguisher and used it on the burning man. The man clearly showed burns on his legs, but nothing life-threatening.

Butler-Kronen was afraid. "What…what…what do you want from us? Is it money, as we can give you money?"

"We want you to stop enslaving our children. Are you not listening?"

Tim, feeling a sense of urgency, nervously texted Brett about his location, who was on the scene, and what was happening, but Brett had yet to answer. Tim then checked Brett's phone locator and noticed what geographical part of DC he was in. It looked like an alley. Tim started to call Howard when Brett called him.

"Tim, I can meet you at the office or wait until tomorrow for my report."

"No way, Brett. You're close to Twins All Night Cafe on 15th Street NW. I'll meet you there in twenty minutes. Have your thoughts together. I'm on my way."

***

The next morning, Howard, Tim, and Brett were seated at Marino's small conference table, while Marino sat at his desk looking at the handwritten document from Brett.

"What?" was all Marino could say when he read Brett's report. His surprise was evident, and it set the stage for the confrontation that was about to unfold.

"What possessed you to follow that vehicle without prior approval or backup? Did we not teach you anything about teamwork?"

Brett felt the weight of his mistake. He also thought the scolding from Tim would have sufficed, but he was wrong. He was also wrong about the length of the lecture he had to endure from Howard. Now, Marino was putting him through the wringer. Damn, this was worse than his parents, he thought. However, regardless of how he felt, he was not about to let his report go unnoticed.

Howard and Tim respected Marino's leadership. They knew his steadfast rule regarding approval and backup was the type of stern talk Brett required. This assurance in Marino's leadership made Brett feel secure, knowing that Marino's belief in teamwork and his care for their safety was of prime importance.

"I know the report is handwritten." Brett stammered, "but it will be a document as soon as this meeting is over."

All three men nodded their heads. Tim gave Brett the "go ahead" nod.

"Since I was on Butler-Kronen detail, my two days following him and his vehicle turned up nothing to raise a flag or eyebrow. I decided to change my M-O and follow him last night. I did not know the vehicle would end up in an alley. I recognized the three men besides Butler-Kronen in the car—Conrad Donahue, CEO of Donahue Tobacco, Philip Branson, CEO of Branson Flour, and Father Stanley Fitzgerald of the Christian Orphanage."

The men in the room were surprised by the planned hit. Brett continued.

"I waited outside Gates and Gardner Steakhouse for almost two hours, when I saw the two Black men grab the driver and throw him into the trunk of another car. I followed to see where their next gathering would be. I did not anticipate that the vehicle would pull into an alley. I also did not expect the two Black men wearing masks to carry all four men into a completely abandoned garage. I deduced the men were unconscious because they were not moving, so they must have been given some sedative while in the vehicle. The Black men then tied each of the men to chairs, poured a liquid on their pants legs, and while waiting for the men to come to, they took pictures of them. I then texted Tim to tell him the situation, but the men came to, and I couldn't read their lips or hear the conversation. I know that Butler-Kronen said something that must have come off as arrogant to the men because then one of the Black men used a lighter to Father Fitzgerald's pants and robe and they lit up like the Fourth of July. His screaming was detectable even through the thick glass. The other Black man quickly doused the fire with an extinguisher."

He paused. "When those Black men were departing, I ducked behind a trash container, making sure they didn't spot me. They ran to the street, where a dark color car was waiting. The abandoned Mercedes was left in the alley. The men in the garage untied their ropes and dashed outside. They assisted the limping priest to the car, his robes stained with blood and burn holes. Someone hopped into the driver's seat, the others jumped into the back and the car sped away. I then walked to my car and drove to the Twins All Night Cafe on 15th Avenue NW to meet Tim and transfer the occurrence on paper, which you just read."

Marino sat back in his seat. He was left speechless for a moment, processing the situation.

"Howard," Marino began while looking at his computer screen, "let's check on the good Father, see what we can learn, aside from religion. Yamamoto, have Waverly find out everything about these two Back men, oh, and have Callahan revisit the Osmans before they send her the next set of photos."

***

Butler-Kronen's companions in the vehicle wanted immediate answers, but first, they had to get the Father to the ER. He screamed more about staff pulling the singed clothing from his skin than when treating his burns. Afterward, a nurse doused the Father's burns with cool water for about ten minutes, then wrapped the areas with a sterile bandage. Once the hospital recorded his side of the story for their records, Father Stanley Fitzgerald was well enough to leave.

Father Fitzgerald had sent for his driver, one he knew, so his ride back to the orphanage was undisturbed. Conrad Donahue, as did Philip Branson, needed a meeting with Butler-Kronen the next morning. Father Fitzgerald bowed out. Butler-Kronen wanted to know how they got to the driver…again.

***

It took the Arundel County Sheriff's Department only a day to find Butler-Kronen's security driver. He was tied to a tree in a field two miles south of Baltimore. Except for the bloody nose and swollen lips, he was alive.

Before he quickly resigned from the Kronen Group, he told his supervisor that while he was waiting for Butler-Kronen and his guests to leave the restaurant, he was dragged out of the car by two Black men. He fought back, but a third party put a bag over his head and threw him into the trunk of a car. Some aerosol was sprayed in his face, and the next thing he knew, he was tied to a tree in the middle of nowhere, screaming at the top of his lungs for someone to help him.

***

Dennis Kelvin obtained Gwen Casey's name and address through the Division of Unemployment Insurance in Baltimore. Callahan drove to the address given to her. The brownish grass surrounding the tiny house looked like it had just been mowed. The house needed painting, but the two wicker chairs on the porch looked inviting. An elderly, slim, Black man with fading freckles and reddish-gray hair came out on the porch as Callahan parked the car in front of the house.

"You must be Agent Callahan, yes?" he asked, scratching his head, in what was surely a unique experience for him.

Callahan bobbed her head and showed the man her FBI credentials.

"Never seen an FBI person before," he said, "especially a woman, but come on in, my daughter is waiting for you."

Gwen Casey, a small but solidly packed woman with freckles and red hair, greeted Callahan with a firm handshake. Callahan found this greeting surprising, but then she realized Gwen had much to say, adding an element of intrigue to the encounter.

"First of all, how did you get my name?" Gwen asked as she gestured toward the living room sofa.

"From Unemployment. I'm just talking to everyone who was released from Donahue Tobacco and tried getting unemployment in the past two years."

Casey seemed secure with the answer. "I ain't getting unemployment even though I have tried twice. They said DT has an 'at will' contract with all employees, saying no matter what, they can fire us for no reason and we can quit for no reason. They told Unemployment that I quit. They were lying 'cause I did not quit."

"Why *did* you leave, Miss Casey?" Callahan asked.

"I am going to tell you the truth now and I don't care who knows it. DT has kids working for them after all our employees leave for the day. Do you know how I know? I missed my bus one day and had to go to the bathroom, so I went through the shipping department 'cause it was a shortcut. I saw little kids working on boxing cigarettes and loading them in trucks. Little kids!!"

"Miss Casey, how old would you say the kids were?"

"Maybe eight, maybe ten. But they was kids. There had to be about twenty of them working."

"Were there any adults around?"

"I didn't see any, which was strange 'cause these children seemed to know what they were doing. Anyway, I ran to the bathroom and then went and caught the next bus. The next morning, I went by the shipping department, and adults were working on the assembly line. But the next day, I went to the shipping department after I got off work and saw a busload of kids going into the shipping department. Little kids. I told Gloria, who I thought was my friend in HR, about what I saw, and she said I was confused—that DT don't hire no children to work for them."

"What happened after that?"

"I had lunch with some of my friends in assembly and shared what I had seen. I was determined to report this to HR. However, when I got to HR, Gloria's boss, Mister Arthur Davidson, was waiting for me with my last paycheck. He told me that my services were no longer required. I felt betrayed. It was clear— this was retaliation."

"How are you getting by financially?"

"Right now, my pension from Streets&San, and my daddy's pension from the gas company, are keeping us okay. I worked at Donahue for only six years, so I'm still looking for a job. I'm only fifty-six. You don't have any openings at the FBI, do you?"

Callahan hid her smile. "I'm not sure. However, Miss Casey, would you be willing to tell your story about the children working at Donahue to my boss in DC? We are working on a case that might involve Donahue Tobacco."

"Oh Lordy, yes. I'm ready to do whatever. I'd like to show Donahue Tobacco what retaliation really looks like."

***

Baltimore SA David Martinez showed up at his first day at Branson Flour wearing faded jeans, a flannel shirt, and worn tennis shoes. He had been hired almost immediately in the Packaging and Distribution department. He and others on the assembly line packaged the flour in bags of various sizes. The bags were then boxed and sent to supermarkets, restaurants, commercial bakeries, and food producers. The black logo of Branson Flour, now adorned with the Mila apparatus by Ahmad Waverly, was a unique addition to Martinez's four shirts, much to his wife's dismay when it came to laundry time. He was allowed two fifteen-minute breaks and a thirty-minute lunch. When he asked if he could work overtime because his wife was expecting a baby soon, he was told "there is no overtime, sorry."

Martinez reported daily to Ahmad and Howard, then Millhouse, his boss. Nothing seemed out of line even when Martinez asked why there was no overtime allowed. The answer came back several times the same way—"many employees, so don't need anyone working overtime."

***

After five weeks of therapy, Joel Stover's mental picture had become somewhat clearer. Shari and Gina were greatly relieved, a feeling that reassured them about Joel's progress. His feelings of remorse for involving many, many people with his gun were evident. However, Joel was grappling with conflicting emotions and believed he did not deserve the attention he was getting. He wanted to get out of prison and back to his life. He wondered if his career would take a turn for the worse.

The doctors recommended that Joel continue therapy for several months, possibly up to a year. This news was disappointing to Joel because it meant he had to stay in the hospital. Shari outlined the goal of maintaining a positive outlook. She also stressed the importance of Joel's commitment to the therapy, as it was crucial for his recovery and his future with his employer…who she was told would welcome him back.

Several days later Joel was quite surprised when his visitor turned out to be Carol Watson. He felt he couldn't face her, so he quickly left the visiting area. Carol understood. She also knew that guilt crept into his conscience—a good sign to her. She would visit again.

***

When John Fleischman walked into Marino's conference room, the conversations ceased, leaving a thick silence in the air. Fleischman's gaze swept around the room at the twelve agents assembled, and he shook his head so that everyone knew he was about to shell out bad news. He didn't disappoint.

"Although Miss Casey and Mr. Osman's statements seem legitimate, the DOJ doesn't feel it's concrete proof to hand out warrants. They're on our side, still, they need actual proof that underage children are being labor trafficked by Donahue Tobacco, Branson Flour, and Christian Orphanage—*actual proof*, as in pictures, video, or audio. If the accusations ring true, the ramifications are that these businesses will close, the orphanage will fold, 1120 people will be out of a job, and sixty-two children's lives will be placed in the hands of the Federal government. Is there anyone in this room who doesn't understand what I am saying?"

No one said a word.

"Good, get at it." He then walked out of the room.

"Whoa" was all Howard could think about. *Fleischman had something meaningful to say. Shocker!*

Howard glanced at Marino, who looked eerily composed. Marino got up from his chair and walked over to the window and peered out. After a minute, he turned to the group.

"Waverly, you have some work to do because we need video. Lee and Martinez, we need video. Callahan, get that priest on video. Hamilton, stay on Butler-Kronen and record all audio. Kelvin, get me anything on Misters Donahue and Branson and Father Fitzgerald. At this time, all of you report your daily findings to Yamamoto. Howard, Frank, and Terrence, in my office."

Unfortunately Howard felt he and the others were being manipulated because they had to prove quickly beyond a shadow of a doubt that the three concerns they were chasing were justifiably being accused of child labor trafficking. Howard and Frank sat on Marino's sofa while Millhouse sat at his conference table.

Marino wasted no time. "As far as John's sermon goes, he's right. It's not surprising to any of us that child labor trafficking is notoriously underreported. The victims and survivors are afraid to come out of the shadows. These pieces of dirt we ironically call humans use violence, threats, lies, and other forms of coercion to force these children to work against their will. The three establishments are staring at us in the face."

Marino paused, went into his drawer and got a cigar out of its humidor. He ran it across his upper lip.

"I understand John's wife plays golf with Butler-Kronen's wife, so trespass gingerly, but trespass."

Later in the day, David Martinez urgently reported to Millhouse that he had met an employee at Branson Flour who had been referred to him by Amadi Osman. Millhouse, in turn, promptly called Howard to discuss the matter.

"Let me get this straight, Millhouse. Did this person Martinez never met put himself out to a stranger and tell him about the kids working after hours for Branson Flour? This is quite unexpected."

"Yes, it is. Also, the children are all from Christian Orphanage for Indigenous Children."

"Wow, that is news. Why do you suppose he approached Martinez? He's only been there a week."

"*She* approached Martinez because her fiancé is in graduate school with Amadi Osman, and Osman told her it was safe to talk to him. She also said she had a video of the children working there."

"Wow, again. Will this person talk with us?"

"I'm afraid not. She is the sole breadwinner in a single-parent home. However, she can give Martinez the tape."

PART THREE

Callahan met with Howard and Frank in Howard's office. She handed a document to Frank and then to Howard, who sat at Howard's conference table. Both men glanced at the various bullet points, but Callahan dispensed the information.

"Based on statements I took from four retired members of the Christian Orphanage for Indigenous Children, Father Stanley Fitzgerald is not a priest or father at all."

Howard's eyes widened in shock at the unexpected revelation.

"Mrs. Dina Bruce, an Indigenous woman and retired maintenance worker at the Orphanage, recalled when 'Stan' Fitzgerald first came to the orphanage about twenty years ago. He was probably about forty years old and an out-of-work farmhand hired to care for the orphanage's grounds, including the cemetery. When the real Father Bennet died three years later, after serving as the priest for the church and orphanage for twenty-four years, the orphanage's future was uncertain. No one came forth even after six months to take over the church and orphanage, and Mrs. Bruce believes that no one ever informed the district of Father Bennet's passing. Anyway, Stan Fitzgerald became Father Stanley Fitzgerald."

Frank looked confused. "The workers just let Fitzgerald take over as a priest?"

"According to Mrs. Bruce, yes. After three years of watching Father Bennett, Fitzgerald knew he could conduct the services, communion, and baptism and supposedly knew the Bible. He told the flock that Father Bennett wanted him to take over. At the time, all the workers at the church and orphanage were Indigenous or Mexicans—he was a white man, so he fell right in place.

"However, after the absence of two quarterly financial reports and no answer from Father Bennett, a member of the Diocese of Baltimore took a trip to the church. Once the member realized Bennett had died and had been buried, he also realized they had no other priest to send to the area, so they made Fitzgerald a Deacon. After a year, though, the church withdrew their financial support based on the idea that the government or a Tribal entity would take over the orphanage. That didn't happen, so Fitzgerald, with a modicum of power, became financial buddies with Donahue Tobacco and Branson Flour—delivering children for their profitable bottom line."

"How old is this Mrs. Bruce?" Frank asked.

"I would say definitely in her sixties."

"So, old enough to have known both Fathers. Good work, Callahan," he remarked.

"Thanks, Frank."

***

After seven days of anticipation, Ahmad finally devised something he thought might appease Marino. Howard, always intrigued by Ahmad's creations, called the troops into Marino's conference room without viewing the invention beforehand.

Ahmad took out of his trusty backpack a belt buckle that mirrored the one he was wearing.

"That's it?" Marino said, on the verge of boredom.

"Okay," Ahmad began, "don't be so quick, Director. I noticed that the uniforms at Donahue and Branson required a belt. Milo, or minuscule interlocking operator, will be your belt buckle. My Milo has just recorded everything that happened five minutes before the start of our meeting. Shall we take a quick look?" he said with a smirk.

Ahmad then casually detached the buckle from the belt, connecting it to a USB cord and his laptop. On Ahmad's screen, the video showed Ahmad navigating the room and captured a couple of light-hearted jokes between Howard and Tim. So, video and audio were a hit.

"Waverly." Marino smiled. "You're good. However, what are the caveats?"

"Well, there are three. One, the buckle can't get wet. Two, the buckle cannot be near a heat source—fire, stove, microwave, grill, etc. Three, although it can record hours of video, Milo is running on lithium power, so the lifespan is only eight hours—sorry."

"Wow," Howard proclaimed. "Okay, so this means, Agents, you start your engines when you know you have only eight hours to operate. Right, Ahmad?"

"Yes, Howard. Look at this way, Kevin and David. You don't have to hand wash your shirts anymore."

***

Joel Stover had his four days in court. He nixed having a jury trial and opted for a judge's decision based on his attorneys believing a bench trial would be quicker. The court-ordered psych evaluation revealed Stover was unable at the time to distinguish between right and wrong. Although District

Court Judge Lauren Cannon noted the forty-two character witnesses in the court, including CIA Officer Liling Xu and FBI Special Agent Katherine Perry, and Stover's employers, she had harsh words for Stover.

"Mr. Stover, please stand and face the bench. You admitted to planning the possible kidnapping of Mrs. Carol Watson. Regardless of the pain and suffering you caused Carol Watson's family, friends, and so many others in the room, I will say I have been on the bench for twenty-four years, and I have never seen this many people, including the victim, come together to save someone's life from ruin as they have for you."

She paused and looked around the courtroom. "The fact remains, however, Mr. Stover, the concern of this bench is the display of the firearm, although legally licensed and purchased, you intended to intimidate, coerce, or threaten someone. You demonstrated a callous disregard for the sanctity of human life. Since you pleaded guilty and based on the laws handed down by the Commonwealth of Pennsylvania, I am therefore sentencing you to twenty-two months in the Pennsylvania Department of Corrections for brandishing a firearm for intimidation, coercing, and threatening."

Stover's knees buckled a bit but he remained standing.

"However, in agreeing with your attorney and the US Attorney, I am reducing that time to sixteen months as an in-patient and six months as an out-patient for mental wellness at a Pennsylvania mental health facility. If, after twenty-two months, the psych evaluations return to me with a positive recommendation of your no longer being a safety threat or concern to society, the US Attorney will downgrade your crime to a Class B misdemeanor, with time served. Mr.

Stover, do you understand that these current felony charges could have resulted in a permanent criminal history, including months in the county jail or *years* in prison?"

"Yes, I understand."

"The possible downgrade to a Class B misdemeanor should provide some relief for your mental health. Use these twenty-two months wisely, Mr. Stover."

Shari and her daughter Gina breathed a sigh of relief, their hope for Joel's recovery shining through. Joel would be in good hands, Shari thought, with enough resources to help him tackle his demons. After hugging and kissing his mother and sister, the bailiff escorted Joel out of the courtroom.

Judge Cannon looked at Shari in a way that demonstrated that she also shared their hope for Joel's recovery through therapy. Although the Judge chose to hear from only a third of the witnesses, all those gathered in the courtroom smiled broadly as they headed out of the courtroom. And all seemed pleased upon hearing Joel's verdict. Carol Watson and Shari Stover shared a mother's smile of relief.

***

Kevin wondered why he hadn't seen Chester Davis all day. His Chinese associate told him "he was let go because 'they' said he couldn't cut the mustard." Kevin believed he was let go because higher uppers thought he had loose lips. He would find Chester and get the real story. Kevin's day dragged on without the good-natured Chester Davis he had come to know in only three short weeks. Meanwhile, his Milo was capturing video, and because he was pissed due to Chester's untimely liberation, he wandered over to the shipping department as soon as he left work for the day. *What are they gonna do—fire me?*

This day Milo captured a group of twenty-two kids, possibly aged eight to ten, disembarking from a bus graced with the Christian Orphanage for Indigenous Children logo.

"What are you doing here?" Plummer's voice boomed, demanding an answer.

Kevin recognized the voice without turning around. "I'm not doing anything. It's freaky to see so many kids working. Is this some kind of internship program for them?"

"Yeah, it is," Plummer answered. "I believe I told you this department was not your responsibility. Why are you here?"

"I saw these kids on my way to catch my bus. I was curious. What's your problem?"

"My problem, Mr. Lee, or whatever your real name is, I don't believe you are here to work. Am I correct?"

"What's that supposed to mean?"

"It means you are here to spy on us."

Suddenly, Plummer brandished a weapon and pointed it at Kevin, causing a moment of shock and tension.

"Let's take a little walk, shall we, Mister Lee?"

With the gun firmly pressed against Kevin's back, both men walked to the HR department, where Arthur Davidson was still in his office, unaware of the unfolding drama.

When they stepped into his office, Davidson was struck by a wave of shock at the sight of both men, especially one holding a gun.

"What the hell is going on here, Plummer?" he yelled.

"Sit down, Arthur. I believe we have a mole here."

Kevin sighed. "What is a mole?"

"Don't play innocent," Plummer warned, his voice low

and menacing. "You've been lurking around our shipping department, and I want to know why."

"He's been doing what?" Davidson's voice tone echoing in the small office.

"He's been seen watching the shipping department even though I told him it was off-limits. So why is he still around? Snooping, that's what he's doing."

Davidson's smile faded from his face. "Search him. See what he has on him."

"Whatever you're looking for is not on me," Kevin proclaimed. "I have no idea what you guys are doing. What kind of company are you running here?"

Plummer meticulously and thoroughly searched Kevin's clothing and beyond, his determination unwavering. He was beginning to doubt his suspicions, but his contrasting personality told him there was something up with this Chinese fellow.

"Just his wallet, state ID with his name Kevin Lee, his bus pass and some money. Nothing else."

"What is going on here?" Kevin demanded, his voice echoing in the dimly lit warehouse office.

"It seems to us," Davidson interjected, "that you are one curious fellow. Why is that, Mr. Lee? What are you looking for?"

"You are right, Mr. Davidson. However, my mother would just say I'm nosey. If you don't want me in this section, I won't be in this section—I just want to know why little kids are here. To do what?"

Plummer jumped in. "As I told you, Lee, they are part of a learning experience. Learning how shipping departments run."

"For what reason would a little kid care about how a

shipping department runs—it's not like they can work for at least five to eight years."

Kevin thought he had overstepped his boundaries this time as Davidson looked at him strangely.

"Where'd you come from, Lee? Who sent you?"

Davidson's suspicion hung in the air, leaving everyone intrigued about Kevin's true intentions. He then looked in a file cabinet and found Kevin's file. He perused it and put it back.

"Calvin Wong helped me get the job. What are you waiting for me to say?"

Davidson continued to stare at Kevin. "Yeah, we know Wong, you're probably legit. We don't give warnings here at Donahue, but we will this time, Lee—stay out of shipping."

Kevin left the warehouse without Plummer or Davidson seeing him take the shortcut through the shipping department. At least twenty children were boxing cigarettes and loading them into trucks. He hoped Milo was still operating and that he captured video and audio. *Please God let this happen.*

***

David Martinez could not get an honest answer from anyone at Branson Flour regarding the rule of no overtime. He recalled Kevin Lee mentioning that people would not be forthcoming, and if they were to offer any explanation, it would be succinct or rumored information. Finally, on Martinez's fourth day at Branson Flour, he headed toward the locker room, where a mysterious package was left at his locker. He immediately looked around the locker room—no one. He almost sprinted to the men's room, entered a stall, and looked inside the package. He smiled, placed the package in his backpack, punched out for the day, and got on his bus toward his car, parked two miles away.

***

Deborah Kenwood, ER nurse at Baltimore General, received approval from her supervisor to put in writing that she submitted three police reports in the past twelve months to the Baltimore Police regarding what she believed was child abuse emerging out of the Christian Orphanage for Indigenous Children. Sergeant Cedric Perlman was in charge of the case.

Gwen Casey, under oath, would attest to witnessing at least twenty underage children working at the Donahue Tobacco manufacturing plant on three separate occasions in the past nine months. She would further state that these children were seen disembarking from a bus affiliated with Christian Orphanage.

Amadi Osman, in a display of remarkable courage, would solemnly affirm that he was coerced by two individuals to retract his statement to the Baltimore police about underage children working for the Kelsy-Wahauser Foundation. His refusal led to a violent assault, resulting in injuries that necessitated hospitalization. Sergeant Cedric Perlman was in charge of the case.

***

Brett Hamilton spent the entire day following and recording Mitchell Butler-Kronen's movements in his black Mercedes. It wasn't until about two hours into his mission that he noticed a persistent presence of a nondescript dark blue

Buick. Brett decided to investigate and texted Tim the license plate and found out that the Crawford Private Investigations Agency was registered and licensed in Maryland, DC, and Virginia. Tim then ordered Brett to find out who was listed as a driver. When Brett gave Tim the news, Tim's voice was tense as he asked the question.

"Are you absolutely sure, Brett, it was the Executive Vice President having his CEO followed?"

"Yes, Tim," Brett answered. "I went to the agency and after displaying my credentials, I asked who belonged to the car I thought was following me. The agency owner and manager, Paul Crawford, showed me the file that listed his two security details and who they were contracted to follow for three weeks—Mitchell Butler-Kronen. The contract was signed by Gavin Henderson, the Executive Vice President at Kronen Group."

"Well, this is a turn in the bend we did not see coming," Tim proclaimed.

"Brett, follow that car and see where it parks at the end of the day."

"Got ya, Tim."

***

Howard, Frank, and Millhouse were each wondering how to pull in Baltimore Police Sergeant Cedric Perlman without his knowledge of their suspicion that he was a critical player in the child trafficking business. They got lucky— Gerry Kramer, Millhouse's boss, played softball with Perlman's captain.

According to Kramer, he would vouch for Captain O'Malley's reputation until the day he died but he had to have absolute facts; they would have to bypass Fleischman so Marino could be in the meeting with him, and they would have to sting Perlman, who might roll over on Donahue, Branson, and possibly Butler-Kronen to get a probable sentence reduced or waived.

That was a big "but" as far as Howard was concerned. However, the men were ready to proceed.

***

Joel Stover was taken aback to find Carol Watson standing before him. Her name was not among the three visitors he had listed. How had she managed to bypass the strict security? He was on the verge of retreating to his room when Carol's voice pierced the air.

"Joel, we need to talk. You need information only I have to help you look forward to tomorrow. Please, Joel, have a seat."

Joel looked at the guard, nodded to him, and took a seat.

Carol took this time to save his life. "Fourteen years ago, I was in love with my then husband, John Mason. He was an FBI Special Agent in the Chicago Field Office for ten years. He earned many awards at that time because he was honest, straightforward, and went by the book. He made me understand that the truth has no versions."

Joel's hands trembled as he struggled to process the shocking revelation. His mind was a whirlwind of conflicting emotions. His eyes were filled with a mixture of shock, disbelief, and anger. He couldn't bring himself to look at Carol, but her words pierced through his defenses.

"Joel, look at me. I was in love with John Mason. We went to college together. We had a son together, and we were

139

working on the rest of our lives together when he was murdered at age thirty-seven. Not killed, but murdered at the hands of two CIA officers and two FBI agents, colleagues, who knew him. One of these colleagues was your father."

Joel looked out the window.

"Joel, look at me," she said calmly. "Your father and his partner, David Snell, decided money was the reason for their joy. Money, Joel. My husband, John Mason, and a *decorated* retired army veteran, Carl Sunderland, were out to prove that the problems plaguing the President of the United States were all fabricated by several US Senators who hired two CIA and two FBI to do their dirty work in getting rid of the president. Do you know why? Because the president did not want any more war-related armaments built!"

Joel sat up straight in this chair. "I don't understand what you are hinting at?"

"Joel, I am not hinting at anything. These weaponry contract companies owned these senators. To keep their seats, they felt no alternative except to get rid of the president and work with the vice president, who would become president and who was in their corner. These are all facts that you now have to absorb to move on. Your father and David Snell kidnapped me and my son because they believed we had a tape with incriminating evidence on these two senators. Your father, whether it was intentional or not, shot me in the abdomen, and I was in a coma—a coma—for four weeks. My son, who is also your age, was ten at the time and thought that he was going to lose his mother, too. As you can see, I pulled through, but it took me another six months to feel alive."

Joel sat without blinking as Carol continued her message.

"You say Howard Watson and I messed up your and your family's life when your father went to prison? He messed up my life too—I was no longer a wife, could no longer teach in the town I loved, my son became fatherless, and yes, we too had to move to another city to rid ourselves of the always present press flying over our every move like vultures. Your father ruined not only the lives of his own family with his greed, but also our lives and the lives of Carl Sunderland's family."

She paused. "If anyone emerged from this as a hero it was your mother, Shari, who was determined to save you, and your sister. Mull over that, Joel. Reflect on the impact of those events. Talk to me when you get out."

Carol then got up, and after relinquishing her visitor's pass, retrieved her phone, keys and purse outside the room, then exited the state mental health facility.

***

Kevin rushed off the bus and made a beeline for his parked car. He drove straight to the office where the team was waiting for him. It didn't matter that Marino had never experienced the joy of fatherhood, he was deeply affected by the evidence of child labor, feeling a profound sense of responsibility. The Milo video, the videotape in David Martinez's possession, and the employees' and nurses' testimonies all painted a dark picture. The potential findings of Howard's and Frank's investigation into the police sergeant could be a turning point for the US Attorney's office. Callahan would work on Father Fitzgerald.

Father Stanley Fitzgerald was confronted with irrefutable evidence and folded like a cheap suit. All

Callahan did was present her FBI credentials and point out that her unit had video and audio recordings of all the victims under the age of fourteen being transported by his Christian Orphanage vehicles daily to Branson Flour and Donahue Tobacco for labor. She also clarified that "Section 1584" does not require proof of force, threats, fraud, or coercion for *minors* to be engaged in labor trafficking. The implication meant fifteen years in prison…for each minor.

Fitzgerald insisted on having his attorney present and was ready to provide information because he was deeply concerned about avoiding prison. Callahan couldn't guarantee this. But, she emphasized that his exploitation of the children's trust, their belief in him, and their faith-based setting would probably lead to his time behind bars.

However, she had a plan for him to consider.

***

Sergeant Cedric Perlman, a trusted Black man in the community, and Father Fitzgerald, the respected leader of the local church, were meeting in Father Fitzgerald's small dining room at the church. They were discussing the upcoming new crop of orphanage kids and how they would get them into Branson Flour and Donahue Tobacco. To the surprise of both men, Amadi Osman interrupted the meeting.

Sergeant Perlman jumped to his six-foot stature. "What are you doing here?"

"I'm sorry, do we know each other?" Amadi asked insincerely.

Fitzgerald stared at Amadi's belt buckle. He then asked leading questions. "Is there something you need or want, young man?" he asked.

"Yes, I just want this cop, this Sergeant Perlman, to stop having me harassed and bullied because I know all the details about his and your involvement in child trafficking," Amadi's voice was trembling with anger and fear.

"What in the world are you talking about, Osman?" Perlman's voice rose, filled with anger. "How is it that you know my name, Sergeant Perlman? I didn't give it."

"We know all about you and your kind, Osman—always running to the police, always getting others involved with believing your stories about child exploitation. We heard you were beaten up because of your loose lips, but I see that hasn't stopped you from stepping over the line this time."

"How do you know I was beaten up, Sergeant? I never filed a complaint."

Blood rushed to Perlman's head before he could think straight. "You little crumb. I will have you thrown into jail just for threatening my life. The Father here will corroborate my testimony…right, Father Fitz?"

Fitzgerald nodded.

"No, Sergeant," Amadi pointed out, a sly smile playing on his lips. "I don't think you're gonna do that. You know why? I have a video of you and Father Fitzgerald meeting with Conrad Donahue, Philip Branson, and Mitchell Butler-Kronen about this very same subject you are meeting with Father Fitzgerald—child exploitation. How about that?"

The revelation hung in the air, a shocking twist in the unfolding drama. Perlman rose from his seat, his face contorted with rage and snatched his handcuffs from behind, the metal clinking ominously. He spit out Amadi his rights, his voice almost venomous.

"What are you arresting me for?" Amadi cried out.

"Threatening me and Father Fitzgerald's lives. What I'll

put together in a criminal base should easily get you ten years in prison."

Amadi's lightbulb clicked. "Okay, okay, okay. If I sign that document that the Foundation wants me to sign, will you let me go?"

Perlman took a moment and then released him. Fitzgerald, who had been holding his breath, finally let it out in a long, relieved sigh.

"You have to stay out of my sight and never involve the Foundation again about anything. Do you understand me, Osman? But if you breathe a word of this child exploitation mess to anyone—anyone, Osman—you'll find a loved one requiring an oxygen mask. You read me loud and clear?"

He then pushed Amadi out of the door. "Now get the hell out of here!"

Amadi, who had landed on the ground, got up, brushed himself off, and smiled all the way to Executive Vice President Gavin Henderson's car which was waiting a half-mile down the road. Both could not contain their smiles as they drove to FBI Headquarters.

Of course Marino was livid. "Listen to me, Callahan, when I tell you this. YOU NEVER INVOLVE CIVILIANS. NEVER! What the hell were you thinking? Why would you give Osman a belt buckle?"

The Director's authoritative tone echoed through the room, demanding attention and respect. His outburst was so unexpected that it stunned everyone in the room, especially Callahan. She had never seen Marino this furious.

"I was thinking of snatching two birds with one stone, Director. I wouldn't let anything happen to Osman. I was listening to the conversation on my Mila apparatus. If Perlman was going to hurt Osman, I would've rushed in and called in backup. But it came out okay in the wash, right?"

"There's no right when we involve civilians, Callahan, there's only prayer. Once this case is settled, I want you on desk duty for sixty days."

Howard glanced quickly at Marino. This was harsh. Marino agreed…reluctantly. "Callahan, thirty days."

She breathed a sigh of relief, as did everyone else in the room.

***

Howard and Frank took a little ride to the office of Branson Flour Company. Philip Branson called his attorney in his office because he didn't trust the FBI on his property without a warrant. Howard told Branson that Father Fitzgerald ran him over with Christian Orphanage's bus.

"That's nonsense," he stammered. "What could you possibly have on me?"

But Branson was confronted with irrefutable evidence a few minutes later by federal authorities who came to arrest him. He slumped in his chair. He was placed in handcuffs and was walked briskly to a waiting vehicle. His lawyer followed behind in his car.

***

When the Feds surprised Sergeant Cedric Perlman at his precinct with a warrant for his arrest, he called out his captain's name. When Captain O'Malley came out of his office, he looked at Perlman almost with disdain. He threw up his hands like they were tied.

***

Christopher Plummer was in Conrad Donahue's office when Donahue's secretary told him on his speaker phone that the federal authorities were outside and wanted to talk to him. At this point, neither man knew of Branson's, Fitzgerald's, or Perlman's arrests.

"What do they want, Shirley?" he asked.

Before she could answer, the feds walked in.

"Mitchell Butler-Kronen, under 18 USC 1584, you are under arrest for allegedly recruiting, enticing, harboring, transporting, providing, or obtaining a person or persons under the age of fourteen for labor or services, through the use of force, fraud, or coercion for the purpose of subjection to involuntary servitude, or slavery. I will now read you your rights."

Christopher Plummer was stunned. The uncertainty of his fate loomed large, a cloud of fear. However, he knew he was next.

***

James Butler-Kronen, Jr., and Gavin Henderson were sitting in Butler-Kronen's den watching a baseball game when "Breaking News" suddenly interrupted the game.

"Today, federal authorities have arrested Mitchell Butler-Kronen, CEO of the Kronen Group, on charges stemming from child labor trafficking. The arrest follows months of surveillance by the FBI, Department of Justice, Department of Homeland Security and the Department of Labor.

"More news at nine."

Both men looked at each other, their smiles indicating surprise and satisfaction.

"I guess you'll be back in the office on Monday, Jim?" Henderson asked.

"I guess so," he answered.

Four months later –

Amadi Osman dropped the fifty children off at their school. In the afternoon, he took the six Indigenous and Mexican children to an afterschool program now located in the Kansas-Stark building. This program, funded by the US Cereal Foundation, Kalaret Tobacco Foundation, and Indigenous Peoples Fund, marked a new chapter in the lives of the sixty-two children transferred from the Christian Orphanage. It provided immediate housing, clothing, and education, offering them a fresh start and a promising future.

Amadi was awarded a key to the city of Baltimore "for his courage and heroic undertaking in saving 62 children from the bowels of labor trafficking." Two months later, Abdo, Aamira, Ibrahim, Amina, Faheem, Georgia Kincaid, and Sandra Callahan watched Amadi cross the stage to receive his Masters in Pharmacology degree from the University of Maryland, Baltimore.

***

Abdo Osman met Gavin Henderson at a cafe outside Baltimore on a beautiful summer evening.

"On behalf of Mr. Butler-Kronen, Jr.," Henderson began, "we want to thank you for your assistance in reducing his son's control in the company which his father started."

He then slid an envelope toward Abdo, who quickly

placed it in the inside pocket of his sports jacket.

Henderson continued. "Mr. Butler-Kronen, Jr. wants you to know how invaluable your assistance was in this matter. You will notice he has provided you with more than promised. He hopes this helps your youngest with any debts he incurred while in grad school."

Abdo, maintaining the formality of the situation, smiled, shook Henderson's hand, got up from his seat, and bid him good evening. Abdo then walked to a vehicle waiting for him. He got in and smiled widely at the two Black muscular men.

"We did well," he said. He then looked in the envelope and gave each man what he had promised to them.

Alexandria, VA

Mark, George, and Lawrence were playing basketball on the driveway when they stopped to let the SUV with Pennsylvania plates pull in. This ended their game, but they were pleased to see little Allen, Jr., now six months old.

Mark ran to the passenger side, taking the baby from Janet's arms without asking. She didn't seem to mind. Knox exited the driver's side, and he and Janet strolled hand in hand toward Howard and Carol's house. Howard was busy barbecuing in the backyard but stopped to hug Janet and shake Knox's hand warmly before handing him a beer.

Baltimore, MD

Kevin Lee walked up the four steps to the frame house, which looked as if it had been over a decade since it had been painted. Chester Davis came out onto the front porch, smiled at Kevin, and invited him inside. After introducing him to his wife, he pointed to the living room sofa. "It was nice of you to call, Kevin. I was wondering if we would ever see each other again. We had some good talks, you and me."

"Yes, we did, Chester. I wanted to see how you're doing. I guess you heard Donahue closed?"

"Oh, my yes. 'Bout time, too. Everybody knew what was going on with them little kids, but folks was just too scared of losing their jobs to say anything. Now, none of 'em have jobs. I was told, though, that unemployment is going to honor everyone's claims, so that's good news. What are you going to do? Go back to the FBI?"

"You know about me, Chester?"

His wife yelled from the kitchen. "They don't call him the 'newsletter' cause he can type."

Both men laughed heartily. Chester's wife brought them some lemonade.

After an hour, Kevin was about to leave and headed to his car. He pulled a package out of the glove compartment and presented it to Chester. "What's this?"

Kevin got behind the wheel. "I thought I would buy you a little gift to remember me by. It's a record by the O'Jays called 'Backstabbers.'"

Chester could not stop smiling.

Washington, DC

Although it was quite early, John Fleischman walked into his conference room to a very awake crowd. In addition to DC personnel, Gerry Kramer, Terrence Millhouse, and David Martinez, all from the Baltimore Field Office, were present.

"I am quite pleased, for the most part," Fleischman began drolly, "that we have eradicated off this earth three businesses that will no longer be on our radar. It's a beginning. All of you performed your duties and tasks to the utmost capabilities, and I, along with Al Marino and Gerry Kramer, am proud to call you the best of the best!"

With that, he signaled to his EA to bring in the coffee and cakes.

The End

Acknowledgments

Although this is a story of fiction, child labor trafficking is very real. Labor trafficking in the United States is a form of human trafficking_where victims are made to perform a task through force, fraud or coercion as it occurs in the United States. Perpetrators of domestic servitude are often well-respected members of their communities and lead otherwise normal lives.

If you suspect someone is a victim of trafficking, you can contact the National Human Trafficking Resource Center at

1-800-373-7888

Getting involved could mean saving a child's life.

- JF

About the author

JoAnn Fastoff is an award-winning author of both fiction and non-fiction books. She has written for numerous publications, has produced three one-act plays Off-Off-Broadway in New York, and produced and directed *Live from the Warehouse,* a jazz program for several PBS affiliates. Ms. Fastoff is an environmental activist, the mother of two adult children and the grandmother of Lia. She lives in Chicago and Mexico.

The Fury is the eighth novel in the Howard Watson Intrigue series. Visit her website at www.JoAnnFastoff.com

www.ingramcontent.com/pod-product-compliance
Lightning Source LLC
Chambersburg PA
CBHW040142160726
48006CB00014B/1588